YOUTH WRESTLING 101

BUILD THE YOUTH WRESTLING PROGRAM YOUR COMMUNITY NEEDS

BY TRE HORTON

Cover design by Jody McAllister
Editor: Savannah Horton, Kase Johnstun
Printed in the United States of America
First Printing: July, 2023
ISBN: 979-8-9881929-0-9

Horton Press LLC.

For my dad, Robert Michaels Horton, whose legacy is embodied in Georgia Wrestling through the impact he had on so many lives.

1971-2020

TABLE OF CONTENTS

FOREWORD - BY KEN CHERTOW

It is with great pleasure that I introduce to you Youth Wrestling 101: Build the Wrestling Program Your Community Needs by Coach Tre Horton. This essential guide, born from decades of experience and wisdom, is designed to give you everything you need to know to either reinvigorate your existing program or to start and grow a successful wrestling program from the ground up.

As a former wrestler, coach, and Olympian, I am no stranger to the transformative power of wrestling. My own accomplishments in the sport include being a three-time Academic All-American, three-time NCAA All-American, two-time Junior National Champion, two-time Junior World Champion, Midlands Champion & OW, and an elected member of the Midlands Hall of Fame, among others. I have worked with athletes on all levels including many well-known athletes like Spencer Lee (three-time National

Champion, five-time All American), Zain Retherford (Silver World Medalist, three-time National Champion), and Quentin Wright (National Champion, three-time All American). These experiences have given me a deep appreciation for the dedication and passion required to excel in wrestling.

I have had the privilege of knowing Tre Horton for nearly 20 years. I met Tre when he was just beginning to learn wrestling, and I have witnessed his steady progress and success, fueled by his consistent hard work, dedication, and passion for the sport. Over the years, Tre has amassed an impressive list of accolades both as an athlete and a coach, showcasing his dedication and passion for the sport. His life experiences as a student, athlete, and coach of boys and girls of all ages make him uniquely qualified to share his thoughts and ideas in this invaluable book.

Tre is currently an Assistant Coach at Life University and the Wrestling Director at Peachtree Ridge, and he has earned numerous coaching and personal achievements over the years. His coaching record boasts three NAIA National Champions, nine NAIA All-Americans, two High School All Americans, four GHSA State Placers, two Youth State Champions, and nine Youth State Placers. In 2021, he was named Gwinnett County Assistant Coach of the Year. His personal record includes being a Brewton Parker College Starter at 157lbs, a third-place finisher at the Georgia College State Championship, a Georgia State Finalist, Georgia State Placer (third), and a four-time State Qualifier, among other notable achievements.

Tre's journey began with the unwavering support of his parents, Robert and Sherry Horton, who not only dedicated themselves to their family but also to the Georgia wrestling community. As the Georgia State Chair, Robert was an impactful leader in the development of wrestling in the state, while Sherry played a crucial role in advancing girls wrestling in Georgia. Together, they were instrumental in starting the Girls State Championship in Georgia and were influential in the growth and development of girls wrestling on a broader scale.

Robert and Sherry's dedication and influence have helped shape the sport in countless ways. Robert also served on USA Wrestling's ad-hoc Associated Styles Committee, where he played a significant role in the expansion of Beach Wrestling, Grappling, Belt Wrestling, and Masters/Veterans Wrestling in the USA. His spirit, although he lost his battle with Covid, lives on through his son Tre and the lessons and inspiration found within the pages of this book.

"Youth Wrestling 101" is a comprehensive guide that covers everything from the basics of building a wrestling curriculum and coaching strategies to the more intricate aspects of program management and community involvement. Coach Tre Horton's insights and expertise, gained from his impressive coaching and personal records, will empower you to build a wrestling program that fosters discipline, perseverance, sportsmanship, and camaraderie among its members.

As you read this book, I encourage you to embrace the lessons and inspiration it offers, whether you are a seasoned wrestling enthusiast or a newcomer to the sport. Coach Tre Horton's passion for wrestling and dedication to its growth are evident on every page, and I am confident that "Youth Wrestling 101" will become an invaluable resource for aspiring wrestling coaches and community leaders alike.

Enjoy the journey and may your wrestling program be a source of pride, strength, and growth for your community.

Sincerely,

Ken Chertow

U.S.A. Olympian
www.kenchertow.com
Gold Medal Training Camp System

HOW TO USE THIS BOOK

Congratulations on picking up this book! You are taking an important step toward building the wrestling program that your community needs, improving your coaching skills, and helping your wrestlers achieve their full potential. This book is your blueprint. Whether you are a college coach, high school coach, or a parent running or looking to run a youth club, you can use this book as a tool for learning and reflection. As a workbook, it is designed to be used as an interactive resource throughout the season. It will provide you with practical tips and advice that you can use to build your youth program and coaching practice, whether you are a seasoned veteran or a rookie coach just starting out.

Many free resources referenced here are available on the website on the following page. Don't forget to swing by the site to pick up your free goodies. I took a lot of time to develop them so you

didn't have to! Follow us at the following page:
www.BuildYourYouthProgram.com.

GETTING STARTED:

This guide is designed to help you develop the skills necessary to succeed as a wrestling Chief Executive Officer (CEO). To get the most value from it, begin by reading each chapter carefully and taking the time to understand the practical advice and strategies presented. It's important to take notes as you read to help you remember key points and ideas.

As you work through the chapters, you'll also find various prompts and activities. These will help you apply what you've learned to your own club. These prompts may ask you to reflect on your own experiences or to brainstorm specific plans to implement the strategies discussed in the chapter.

By engaging fully with the content of the guide, you'll develop a deeper understanding of what it takes to be a successful wrestling CEO. You'll also be better equipped to avoid common pitfalls and to navigate the challenges that come with running a wrestling organization.

Remember, the more you engage with the material presented in the guide, the more you'll get out of it, so be sure to take the time to read each chapter carefully, complete the prompts and activities, and reflect on how you can apply what you've learned to your own club. With dedication and effort, you can develop the skills and knowledge you need to succeed as a wrestling CEO.

CHALLENGE TIME:

In some chapters, you'll find sections called "Challenge Time." "Challenge Time" aims to help you practice the concepts and strategies in each chapter. Please write in them. They include prompts and activities to help you reflect on what you've learned and apply it to your own coaching or your wrestling practice. Take the time to complete these sections; they will help you best understand the material and apply it in a meaningful way.

REFLECTION:

One of the most valuable aspects of this book is the opportunity for reflection. Throughout the guide, you'll find prompts and questions to encourage you to reflect on your own experiences, strengths, and challenges. Take the time to write down your thoughts and insights in the spaces provided. This will help you identify needed areas for growth and improvement, as well as build a deeper understanding of the sport of wrestling.

When I sat down and told my wife that I decided to run for the Youth Director position with the Peachtree Ridge Youth Athletic Association, I had already called up every person I knew who had experience running a program. I wanted to know what challenges I could expect, what challenges they had faced, and what challenges they currently dealt with. What I didn't realize was that as I grew the program, I would spend more time being a CEO than I would be coaching. This is something that the National Wrestling Coaching Association (NWCA) calls their 'CEO' skills at their Leadership Academy every year. Good CEO's have a plan, and you should use the plan to develop your business plan for your program. The takeaway here is twofold: 1) you are most definitely going to end up spending more time as a CEO of the program and should most definitely call everyone, and 2) you should find out everything you can before you get started. I have included so much here to help you get started.

As you work through this guide, remember that it is a tool to support your own learning and growth. Use it in the way that works best for you and your goals. Whether you're a coach, parent, or young wrestler, this book is here to support your journey and help you achieve success in the sport of wrestling. Nobody said the journey was going to be easy, but, with hope, this will make the journey simpler.

If you enjoy reading this book, please take a moment to review it on your platform of choice!

1.

WHAT IS YOUR WHY?

The most important question that anyone who is starting a youth wrestling program should ask themselves is "Why?" Is it for yourself, for your child, or for a family member or friend's child? This shouldn't be an easy answer, and your motivation will be the most crucial part of the process. You've already established that you want to learn more about the process, and your "why" is your motivation. It can affect your outcomes so drastically. Take a moment to write down your answer below, and be honest with yourself. Then turn to the next page and prepare to be challenged.

I am starting a youth wrestling program because...

_____

_____

_____

_____

_____

_____

CHALLENGE TIME

Many people start youth wrestling programs because they or their kids would directly benefit. When we talk about why you are doing it, you should think carefully and critically. So your answer should be unique right? Hopefully, it is. Either way, the challenges that you'll face will be nearly identical.

If you are a high school coach

What happens when you retire? What if you receive an offer you can't turn down from somewhere else? What if you need to start spending more time at home? What happens if you are forced to choose between the two programs?

If you're a parent

What happens when your child says they don't want to do it anymore? What happens when they stop having fun? What if they get hurt? What if it is the children of your friends and family?

Would any of this change your 'Why'? Are you doing this for yourself, them or are you giving back?

GIVING BACK IS MORE THAN JUST A PHRASE.

I would challenge you to take a second look at your "why" statement. Don't let it be something that falls apart because of one change. Let's find a way to include your donation of time to the sport. It's what we call "giving back," and it's critical to the growth of wrestling. We will talk more about that later. If you frame your "why" statement in that context, it's going to take more than just one of those questions to derail you, your movement, and your momentum.

If you feel so inclined to take another stab at it, I've left you a space below. We will get into it a little bit later, but don't include the words champion, championship, or winning.

I am starting a youth wrestling program because...

"It's not the will to win that matters — everyone has that. It's the will to prepare to win that matters."
-Paul "Bear" Bryant

2.

WHAT IS YOUR VISION?

Your "why" statement is going to play a big part in your vision statement. When I took over a wrestling program that had no wrestlers the year before, I had to reevaluate what my expectation of success would look like for my program. Creating a vision of what I wanted the program to be in the future was critical to getting it going.

YOUR VISION IS YOUR ROADMAP.

Having a clear and well-defined vision is crucial to the success of any youth wrestling program. Your vision serves as the foundation upon which your program is built, guiding your decisions and actions, and giving you direction and purpose. It also creates a sense of identity and defines your program's purpose, helping you to communicate its goals to parents, coaches, athletes, and the community.

One common source of confusion when it comes to vision statements is the difference between vision and mission. Your mission is a statement of your program's purpose and goals, while your vision is a vivid and aspirational description of the future state of your program. Your vision should provide a clear picture of where you want to be in five to ten years, what your program will look like, and how it will achieve its goals. It should be a roadmap that you and your team can follow as you work towards your shared goals.

Crafting a good vision statement can be challenging, but it is a critical component of the success of your program. It should include several key elements, such as the purpose and goals of your program, how your program will achieve its objectives, and what your program will look like in the future. When crafting your vision statement, it's important to think carefully about what you want to achieve, who your target audience is, and what you want them to know about your program.

To help you get started, it's a good idea to look at some examples of vision statements from successful companies. Reading and analyzing these statements can help you to get a sense of what makes a good vision statement, how they should be structured, and what they should communicate. By examining other vision statements, you can gain inspiration and insight into what makes your program unique and how to express your goals and aspirations in a clear and concise way.

Example #1
To accelerate the advent of sustainable transport by bringing compelling mass market electric cars to market as soon as possible.

Example #2
To craft the brands and choice of drinks that people love, to refresh them in body and spirit.

When you read those statements, what companies do they make you think of? Did Tesla and The Coca-Cola Company come to mind? What did these statements tell you about what the respective companies do? How concise were they? It's important to think critically about someone else's vision before you craft your own.

When I took the time to write the vision for the Peachtree Ridge Youth Wrestling program, it was taxing. I was unsure of how to make it impactful, reflective of our goals and values while being concise. Eventually I came up with this:

Peachtree Ridge Youth Wrestling

To be the most premier wrestling program in our area by developing individuals who are above reproach, successful in life, give back to their community, and believe in themselves while growing every day.

Given that youth wrestling programs work closely with children, it is important to not only teach the sport but also instill positive values and character development. Therefore, I strongly believe that our program's vision should reflect our core values and emphasize the role of wrestling to promote them. Our ultimate goal is to use wrestling as a vehicle to cultivate a positive and impactful experience for young athletes, helping them develop not only as wrestlers but also as individuals.

CHALLENGE TIME

Creating a strong and clear vision for your youth wrestling program is essential for long-term success. Your vision statement should be an inspiring and concise statement that outlines the goals and aspirations of your program.

To develop your vision statement, start by asking yourself a few important questions.

- Where do you see your program in five to ten years?

- What is the purpose of your program?

- What will success look like at that time?

When drafting your vision, you'll want to consider the unique needs and goals of your community and the athletes you serve.

When developing your vision statement, it's important to take your time and not rush the process. Your statement should be flexible, but it shouldn't be changed too frequently. A clear and consistent vision will help guide the direction of your program and ensure that you stay on track toward achieving your goals.

It's important to remember that a well-crafted vision statement will not only guide your program but will also serve as an inspiration for your athletes, coaches, and community. Make sure that it is communicated effectively to all stakeholders to ensure that everyone is working toward the same goals.

By creating a clear and inspiring vision statement, you'll set the foundation for a successful youth wrestling program that meets the needs of your community and provides meaningful opportunities for your athletes to grow and develop both on and off the mat.

The vision of my program is....

_____

_____

_____

_____

_____

_____

_____

_____

_____

_____

"Champions are made from something they have deep inside them: A desire, a dream, a vision."
- Mahatma Ghandi

3.

WHAT IS YOUR MISSION?

A mission statement, also sometimes called a purpose statement, for some circumstances can be more important than the vision. This is true because a mission statement is reflective of the here and now, rather than five to ten years from now. It answers the question of what, who, why and how the organization goes about accomplishing its vision. Your mission statement is what you will need to draw your starting line, and once you know where you are, you'll be able to draw up goals to get to the end.

BRANDING IS EVERYTHING

Making a mission statement is the first major step to your branding. It is what you will use to distinguish yourself from the other programs in your area and communicate what you are currently doing to make an impact. Check out a few examples below.

San Diego Zoo

San Diego Zoo is a conservation organization committed to saving species around the world.

Girls Scouts

Girl Scouting builds girls of courage, confidence, and character, who make the world a better place.

Some things to notice about those statements. They are clear, concise, inspirational, achievable, and unique. When you are building your mission statement, you have to be able to hit all five of those points.

— Clear: Use language that is intentional but isn't vague. Sometimes it may be better to use simpler language for clarity.

— Concise: Keep it as short as possible while still getting the point across. Don't over complicate it. Long drawn-out statements are difficult to tie into a brand.

— Inspirational: Your mission statement should make people feel inspired. It should make them not only want to see you successful, but be a part of your mission and success. Make it resonate.

— Achievable: Your mission needs to be realistic and something that you can realistically accomplish. Setting goals that are too lofty goals is respectable until you can't achieve them.

— Unique and Memorable: This is pretty simple. Don't copy someone else's mission. Your mission should be unique and memorable so that when people hear it, they immediately think of your brand.

One last thing before you write your mission statement: reread your vision. Remember how in the beginning of this chapter we talked about your starting line? Your vision will give you the direction your mission will need. That framing is what makes a mission statement stand out from the rest. Don't worry about making it perfect the first time. Your mission statement is something that can change over time.

The mission of my organization is...

_____

_____

_____

_____

_____

Writing that mission statement isn't easy, and now that you've done so, you should compare it to other programs in your area. Does your mission statement meet all five of the points? More importantly, when comparing, is it unique? Don't be afraid to change it in the future, especially when we start to evaluate your goals.

"*Outstanding people have one thing in common. An absolute sense of mission.*"
-Zig Ziglar

4.

GOAL SETTING

In previous chapters, we talked about how your vision is where you and your program to be in the future?. Your mission is where you are. When implemented properly, goals form the road or lay the asphalt between your mission and vision. Talking about goals is like talking about opinions. Everyone has one and they may or may not be right. With wrestling, goals are critical to success. When running a wrestling program, they are even more so. We live in a time where so many things are pulling away at our attention, wallets, and energy. It is hard to keep your eyes on the prize but creating goals can help you do just that. Before you can start making goals though, we really need to define the different ways success can look.

SUCCESS ISN'T JUST ABOUT WINNING

Your definition of success shouldn't just be about winning, and it should evolve with your program. You should expect different things all throughout the different stages of your program's growth. You will expect different things from a program where they've been winning back-to-back state championships compared to a program that hasn't won a match in years. With youth programs, you have to really be willing to regularly reevaluate your goals. Yes, I know that being told about goals has got to be the most exhausted topic in coaching, but when you define what the different ways success looks like for your program, being able to create a set of goals becomes easy.

EVALUATE, ADAPT, OVERCOME

Learning how to build individual goals is easy when you follow the SMART method. There are a bunch of different methods out there, but I prefer this method.

— Specific: Define your goals clearly. Clarity in goal setting is important because you and all stakeholders need to be able to understand them.

— Measurable: You need to make sure you include a way to measure the success of your goal. Goals without measure are unachievable.

— Achievable: You need to be able to achieve your goals. If you are going to set a goal for a set number of wins in a month, you have to be able to wrestle at least that many matches.

— Realistic: Set goals that you KNOW that you can achieve. Lofty goals are only respectable when they are achievable.

— Time-based: Every goal should be time based. Goals without timeframes have no urgency because there is no end date.

Example: All wrestlers will attempt an average of two takedowns every match by the end of the month.

When I talk to my kids about goal setting, I make an effort to highlight two additional topics: evaluation and adaptation **Evaluating** and **adapting** of goals is critical to **overcoming** obstacles for success. You have to be willing to regularly take a step back to see your progress toward your goals. Maybe your time frame was too short, or your goal was too lofty? Extending the time frame or adjusting the metric with which you measure your goal are both great ways to adapt your goals so that they are still achievable.

FUNNEL YOUR SUCCESS

Building goals that build into each other tends to foster more success. If you have a new wrestler who sets a goal of being a state champion, is that realistic? It depends. If that is their only goal then not really; however if you set smaller goals that eventually build into your lofty goal, then it isn't too unrealistic anymore.

What are some much smaller things they can do to get there? When we frame it as getting your program off the ground, your vision sets your big goal. Your other goals have to start small. I like to relate it to a funnel. Write down your big goals, then create incremental steps to get there.

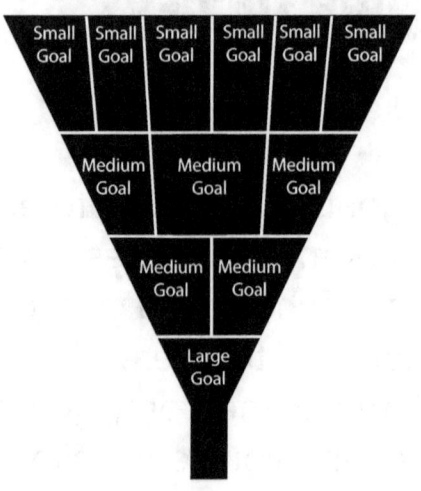

CREATE MOMENTUM

Crafting your goals in a way that funnels creates momentum. The more momentum you have, the easier it will be to get to the next goal.

In the finance world, they call this snowballing. It's a proven success strategy to pay down debt. It's also very effective when used for goal setting. In the funnel, notice how the large goal has multiple medium goals? Engineering your goals this way prevents what I like to call 'the goal block'. Even if you have to adapt one of your goals, you still have other goals that you are consistently working toward that all contribute to the same ending.

CHALLENGE TIME

Now, we need to define what success looks like for you. In the previous three chapters we discussed your why and setting up the mission and vision for your program. For the sake of simplicity, let's set the bar for your measure of success five years from now. What are some examples of ways you could visualize success for your program along the way? Are they in line with your WHY?

Success for me looks like....

_____

_____

_____

_____

_____

_____

Now that you have defined success, you can start making some goals. The vision statement you previously wrote in chapter two should come in handy here.

A large goal for my program would be...

1 _____

_____

Some medium goals for my program would be...

1 _____

_____

2 _____

_____

3 _____

_____

4 _____

_____

5 _____

_____

Getting from where you are to where you want to be should be more than a few small steps. Setting up the small goals is important as it is what gets your program moving.

Some small goals for my program would be...

1 _____

_____

2 _____

_____

3 _____

_____

4
_____

_____

5
_____

_____

6
_____

_____

Remember, nothing you've written for your goals is concrete. That is, unless you make it that way. Always **reevaluate** your goals and **adapt** them if necessary.

"Setting goals is the first step in turning the invisible into the visible."
-Tony Robbins

5.

IDENTIFY YOUR COMMUNITY

Your vision, mission, goals, and why statement are all big parts of making your identity. The thing that makes the biggest impression on how you will implement your program will be your community. Successful programs are made by involved communities. Your program can be quickly broken by a community that does not want to have wrestling or already has a bad taste for the sport. Identifying and being able to respond to your community is going to be a crucial step in getting your program off the ground.

The first and most important question is, what are the boundaries of your community? Is it just a little city? If you target a specific school or cluster, where do the cluster lines stop? Is it county wide, or does it cross county lines? Are the people who work in the area included? Many people choose to do things where they live OR where they work. Who all do you want to include?

The next thing you need to know is who are the people living in your community, and what are their values. Are they a football community? Do they value and push their kids into secondary education or a trade school? If you were to try to summarize who they are into a paragraph, what would it conclude? What type of resources do they have access to? Knowing what they value is important, but knowing who they follow is important too.

That makes identifying the community leaders the next step. They could be school principals, community activists, recreational sports groups, the police chief, religious leaders, or even training center staff. You should know your community better than anyone else.

TEAMWORK MAKES THE DREAM WORK

You can't do this alone. Some of the same leaders in your community could play a large part in building the word of mouth network. Legendary Coach Jim Miller told me a story once about how he would reach out to the leaders in his community when he was coaching at Warburg College. The people he reached out to really brought in the support he needed to get his program going financially and were instrumental in building his fanbase. His book, **Do It Anyway**, is a fantastic read and goes into it a little more. The short version of goes like this: if you can build relationships with those community leaders, then you can start to build a name for your program in your community without your presence. They will talk about what you are doing and you will not even know it.

CHALLENGE YOUR VISION

Once you have identified your community and the leaders within, you can challenge your vision to see if it will meet the needs of the community. For example, If you are in a space where education is prioritized, what will you do to encourage good academics? How will you relate the potential of wrestling paying for part of or all of college? Another example, ff they value other sports like say, football, how will wrestling help them in their sport?

Communicating the benefits of wrestling means being able to build rapport with the community, and you can't do that unless you really understand it.

"Alone, we can do so little. Together, we can do so much."
-Hellen Keller

6.

LOCATION, LOCATION, LOCATION

Finding a place to run your wrestling program is a challenging task if you do not have a facility already. Starting from scratch isn't really viable for most people with the associated high startup costs. Identifying and negotiating for a potential practice facility isn't really talked about mainstream. The amount of funds you have for start up can quickly limit your ability to open your doors. If you already have a facility, ensuring that it is ready for younger age groups is a task in and of itself.

In the last chapter we talked a little bit about finding leaders in your community. Talking to those people may leave you with some insight as to some local options. Successful new programs tend to partner with facilities that have the lowest facility start up costs. What does that mean and what are facility start up costs? Simply put, they are mats, wall pads, rental fees, and any items necessary to keep your wrestlers safe. Finding facilities that have a wrestling mat would be my suggestion. Partnering with the local high school would be the first place I would start.

Partnering with the local high school would be a great way to immediately create   respect for your program. You would immediately have a mascot, support and a fully furnished facility. If the high school coach is really supportive, he will send high schoolers to help coach during the week. Odds are, this won't work if you're running a for-profit youth club unless you have a great relationship with the high school coach. To do that, you'll most likely need to strike out on your own or at the very least partner with a nearby business.

IDENTIFY YOUR OPTIONS

A good starting point for for-profit clubs would be a reputable martial arts gym in the area. They are typically equipped with suitable mats for a beginner program and will welcome the opportunity to have another martial art in their gym that they won't have to manage. You're bringing in potentially new clients and will be there to teach skills to their own clients that they may not have been covering.

Hole-in-the-wall gyms are also a great option. If you have your own mat already or have the funds to purchase one, then they may welcome the opportunity to be able to open another leg of their business in their building (e.g. yoga, mixed martial arts, etc). While you may have to share the use of your mat, it would give you a great place to call home!

Once you have identified potential partners, it is important to evaluate them carefully and negotiate for the best possible terms. When evaluating a facility, make sure to consider factors such as the quality of the mats, the safety of the location, and the availability of parking and restrooms. You should also ask about any additional costs, such as rental fees or equipment maintenance so that you can accurately assess the overall expense of the facility.

When negotiating with a potential partner, it is important to have a clear understanding of what you are looking for and what you can offer in return. Be prepared to present a compelling case for why the partnership would be mutually beneficial and be willing to listen to their concerns and needs. It may also be helpful to research similar partnerships in your area to get a sense of what is standard and what may be negotiable. Ultimately, the goal is to find a partner who is enthusiastic about your program and willing to work with you to create a successful wrestling program that benefits both parties.

"If you wrestle long enough, the wrestling room will start to feel like home. You can eat, sleep, and train all in the same place."
-Tre Horton

7.

WHO WILL YOU PARTNER WITH?

Starting a wrestling program can be a challenging but rewarding undertaking. The most important aspect of getting a wrestling program off the ground is securing sponsorships. Sponsorships can provide financial support and other resources that can help keep your registration costs low so your wrestling program can succeed. In this section, we'll cover the steps you can take to get sponsors for your new wrestling program.

Define your target audience and goals.

Before you start reaching out to potential sponsors, it's important to have a clear understanding of who your target audience is and what your goals for the wrestling program are (we discussed this in chapter two). This will help you tailor your pitch to the needs and interests of potential sponsors.

For example, create a list of all of the local small businesses that other larger sports programs may not have contacted. Are there any restaurants, realtors, or gift shops near by?

Create a sponsorship package.

Once you have a clear understanding of your target audience and goals, it's time to create a sponsorship package that outlines the benefits of supporting your wrestling program. A sponsorship package typically includes the following:

- A cover letter that explains the purpose of the sponsorship package and outlines the benefits of supporting your wrestling program.

- A sponsorship proposal that outlines the various sponsorship levels and the benefits associated with each level.

- Marketing materials, such as flyers or brochures, that showcase your wrestling program and the benefits of sponsorship.

- If you are relaunching a program, a media kit that includes information about your wrestling program, such as the number of participants, the demographics of your audience, and any notable achievements or milestones would be beneficial. You never know who has had kids participate in the wrestling program in the past who can help you.

Identify potential sponsors

Now it's time to start identifying potential sponsors for your wrestling program. There are several ways you can do this:

- Research companies and organizations that are already involved in wrestling or support athletics in general. These may include wrestling-gear manufacturers, sports-nutrition companies, or local businesses that have a history of supporting sports programs in your community.

- Reach out to other wrestling programs or coaches in your area and ask for recommendations. They may have had success in securing sponsorships and can provide valuable insights and introductions.

- Consider local businesses or organizations that align with the values and goals of your wrestling program. For example, if your wrestling program has a strong focus on community service, you may want to reach out to businesses or organizations that also prioritize community involvement.

For example, create a list of all of the small hole-in-the-wall businesses that other larger sports programs may not have contacted. Are there any restaurants, realtors, or gift shops near by?

Hot Tip: You may want to focus on securing a sponsorship from a local company that produces wrestling gear or apparel to help bring down the costs of the gear. It could be your biggest expense!

Make a list of potential sponsors

Once you've identified potential sponsors, make a list of them and prioritize the companies or organizations that are most likely to be interested in supporting your wrestling program. You can use this list as a starting point for reaching out to potential sponsors.

Contact potential sponsors

Now, it's time to start reaching out to potential sponsors. There are several ways you can do this:

– Email: You can email potential sponsors to introduce your wrestling program and request a meeting or phone call to discuss sponsorship opportunities. Be sure to include a copy of your sponsorship package in the email.

– Phone call: If you prefer to speak with potential sponsors directly, you can call them and request a meeting or phone call to discuss sponsorship opportunities.

– In-person meeting: If possible, it's a good idea to meet with potential sponsors in person to discuss your wrestling program and the benefits of sponsorship. This can be especially effective if you have a strong relationship with the company or organization.

Follow up with potential sponsors

After you've reached out to potential sponsors, it's important to follow up with them to keep the conversation going. This can be as simple as sending a follow-up email or calling to check in to see if they have any questions or concerns. If you haven't heard back from a potential sponsor after a few weeks, it's okay to follow up again to remind them of your request and see if they're still interested in discussing sponsorship opportunities. Remember to be patient and persistent when following up with potential sponsors. Securing sponsorships can be a time-consuming process, and it may take several attempts to get a response from a potential sponsor.

Negotiate sponsorship terms

If you're able to secure a sponsorship, the next step is to negotiate the terms of the sponsorship. This will typically involve discussions around the level of financial support the sponsor is willing to provide, as well as any other benefits they may be able to offer (e.g. advertising, in-kind donations, etc.).

It's important to be clear about your needs and expectations as a wrestling program, and to be open to negotiating and finding a mutually beneficial arrangement. Don't be afraid to ask for what you need, but also be prepared to compromise if necessary.

Maintain the sponsorship relationship

Once you've secured a sponsorship, it's important to maintain the relationship with your sponsor. This can include:

- Providing regular updates and reports on the progress of your wrestling program.

— Acknowledging the sponsor's support in your marketing materials and at event.

— Inviting the sponsor to events and matches to show appreciation for their support.

— Offering opportunities for the sponsor to engage with your wrestling program and its participants (e.g. hosting a clinic, sponsoring a tournament, etc.)
By maintaining a strong relationship with your sponsors, you'll increase the likelihood that they will continue to support your wrestling program in the future.

Diversify your sponsorships

It's a good idea to diversify your sponsorships by securing support from multiple sources. This will help ensure that your wrestling program does not rely too much on any one sponsor, making it more resilient to potential setbacks.

Be creative and persistent

Finally, don't be afraid to think outside the box and be persistent when it comes to securing sponsorships for your wrestling program. Consider hosting fundraisers or other events to generate additional support, or reaching out to non-traditional sponsors who may be interested in supporting your program. The more creative and persistent you are, the more likely you are to succeed in securing the support your wrestling program needs to thrive.

FUNDRAISING DOESN'T END THERE

Raising funds via sponsorships is a great way to get your program off the ground. Looking to years two and three, you will want to start looking to create additional streams of revenue for your program. While a lot of people have moved to email based fundraising, I believe that fundraising on the youth level teaches a lot of soft skills. How you choose to go about fundraising is up to you, but I have included a few ideas from successful programs below that the kids can help with.

Fundraising Ideas

– BBQ Plates

– Spirit Wear

– Gourmet Popcorn

– Candy Bars

– Car Wash

– Spirit Night at a Local Restaurant

– Raffle

– Cookie Dough

– Pancake Breakfast

If there is anything I can share, it is that fundraising takes time to become successful. It may take several years for your fundraisers to hit full stride. So don't let their lack of initial success be a deterrent.

"Be happy with what you have while working for what you want."
– Helen Keller

8.

LAY DOWN THE BUDGET

Good money management is beyond important. It can be what breaks your program during the next season. Your budget is what ultimately establishes your registration fees, but it also serves as a general overview of your expenses and income. This section is going to help you walk through how to lay this out and it's going to be a little dry. My suggestion is to do this in a Microsoft Excel Spreadsheet. If you don't have Microsoft Office, then you can use Google Sheets. Either way, I would at the very least do this on a computer for record keeping purposes.

The good news is I have put together a spreadsheet for you already! So this will serve as more of a how-to guide than anything. Before we jump into the sheet, something you should do is start thinking about what you'll be spending money on, and what you'll need at the bare minimum to make wrestling happen. I've created a quick list below to help you get started.

Example Expenses

— Uniforms (singlets, two pieces, t-shirts)

— Coaches Cards (AAU, USA, etc.)

— Background Checks for Coaches

— Chow Box (snacks for the kids at events)

— Tournament Fees (duals or individual tournaments)

— Transportation (will you be taking a bus?)

— Facility Fees

— Scholarships (for registration fees, shoes, headgear, etc)

- Advertising (Flyers and Signs)

- Hotels

- End-of-year gifts

- Coaches Gifts (for additional coaches)

- Banquet Fees

- Awards

You should also think about potential ways you can bring in additional funds. Keeping registration costs low will make your program more competitive. This is especially important in areas where wrestling isn't popular because you're competing against other sports and not just other wrestling programs.

USING THE SPREADSHEET

If you're familiar with Excel, then you may not need this section; however if you aren't, then this will serve as a guide for building it out yourself. The Spreadsheet is on the next page, and is pretty self explanatory being broken down into three sections. The overview, income, and expense sections should serve as an easy way to not only stay organized but a great way to make it so someone can come behind you if ever necessary.

If there are specific changes you want to make, check if I have covered them below. The first step is to rename your budget on the cover sheet! The cover sheet contains a summary of the current year data. You should not change those formulas.

The image on the next page is what the main budget page will look like on the Budget sheet tab.

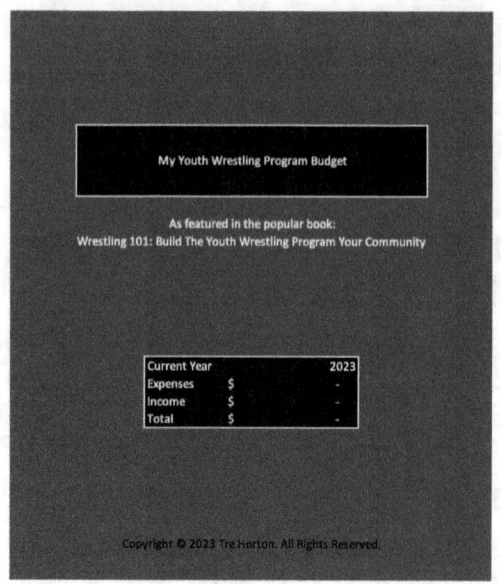

Budget Cover Page

I want to make sure I never lose this...

Save, Save, SAVE! I can't stress that enough. Saving the document in at least two if not three different places is the best thing you can do. If you use the same file for year-over-year budgeting, then this is even more important!

Place 1: On your computer.

Place 2: Save a copy to a flash drive that you don't always keep connected to the computer.

Place 3: Using a service like OneDrive, Google Drive, or OpenDrive to back it up on the cloud.

I want to tie some income or expenses to the number of kids in the overview section...

This requires a simple formula. For any line item you wanted tied to the number of registrations, input the formula below for the quantity.

=D5

This takes the value from the cell where you can change the number of expected registrations (D5) and keeps the value updated.

I have more than income items or expenses...

You can easily add additional rows by selecting a row between the header and the total rows. Then right click it and select 'Insert'. This will add an additional row without messing up any of the formulas.

I want to make another budget for next year in the same workbook...

This is an easy multi-step process. I would first start by making a copy of the sheet you are in.

— Right click the sheet

— Select 'Move or Copy'

— Check the box 'Create a copy' and then select 'ok'

Rename the new sheet using the steps Below.

— Right click the sheet labeled 'Budget'

— Select 'Rename'

— Enter the name you would like e.g. 2022

I have also included a sheet titled 'Historical' so you could copy and paste all of the data (select values only when you paste) so you can track year-over-year expenses, rather than copying the

My Current Budget
Registration Cost $200
Wrestlers 25

REVENUE	Item/Category	Cost per unit	Total Needed	2023 Extended
	Total Player Registration Fees	$ 200.00		$5,000
	Sponsorships	$ 1,000.00		$500
	Donations	$ 500.00		$200
	Apparel Sales	$ 100.00		$100
	Fundraising			$1,000
	Spring Wrestling			$1,000
TOTAL REVENUE				$7,800

FIXED EXPENSES	Item/Category	Cost per unit	Total Needed	Extended
	Facility Rentals	$ 100.00	10.00	$1,000
	Website	$ 5.00	12	$60
	Marketing & Advertising	$ 1.00	400	$400
	Equipment Rentals (Fixed)	$ -	0	$0
	Referees	$ 2.00	200	$400
	Volunteer Background Checks	$ 10.00	25	$250
TOTAL FIXED EXPENSES				$2,110

VARIABLE EXPENSES	Item/Category	Cost per unit	Total Needed	Extended
	Staff			
	Coaches/Board Shirts	$ 45.00	25	$1,125
	Coaches Cards	$ 45.00	25	$1,125
	AAU/USA/NUWAY Coach Cards	$ 45.00	25	$1,125
	Coaches Certifications	$ 45.00	25	$1,125
	Background Check	$ 45.00	25	$1,125
	Advertising			
	Flyers	$ 45.00	25	$1,125
	Signs	$ 45.00	25	$1,125
	Uniforms and Clothes			
	Uniforms	$ 45.00	25	$1,125
	Shirts	$ 45.00	25	$1,125
	Banquet, Awards and Gifts			
	Academic Awards	$ 45.00	25	$1,125
	Awards	$ 45.00	25	$1,125
	State Placer Awards	$ 45.00	25	$1,125
	Banquet Supplies/Decorations	$ 45.00	25	$1,125
	Coaches Gift	$ 45.00	25	$1,125
	Jr Coaches Gifts	$ 45.00	25	$1,125
	Banquet Funds - Wrestling	$ 45.00	25	$1,125
	Travel Expenses			
	Travel Hotel	$ 45.00	25	$1,125
	Travel Gas	$ 45.00	25	$1,125
	Travel Van	$ 45.00	25	$1,125
	Dualing Expenses			
	Officials	$ 45.00	25	$1,125
	Dual Registration Fees	$ 45.00	25	$1,125
	Scholarship Expenses			
	Shoes	$ 45.00	25	$1,125
	Head Gear	$ 45.00	25	$1,125
	Registration Scholorships	$ 45.00	25	$1,125
	Team Expenses			
	Warm Up Jackets	$ 45.00	25	$1,125
	Warm Up Pants	$ 45.00	25	$1,125
	Storage Boxes	$ 45.00	25	$1,125
	Fees			
	Registration Platform Fees	$ 45.00	25	$1,125
	Subscriptions			
	Platforms	$ 45.00	25	$1,125
TOTAL VARIABLE EXPENSES				$32,625

TOTAL EXPENSES				$34,735
INCOME				-$26,935

Budget Spreadsheet

sheet itself. However you do it, this sheet is yours to customize as you see fit!

Don't forget to swing by www.BuildYourYouthProgram.com to pickup your free program budget template to help you stay organized.

"A budget doesn't limit your freedom; it gives you freedom."
– Rachel Cruze

9.

BUILDING YOUR CULTURE

Culture in a wrestling program is a difficult concept for a lot of coaches to wrap their heads around. Everyone has a wildly different definition of culture as well. My definition tends to be a little more in-depth. I hope that reading this will give you a better understanding of what you want your culture to look like in your program, and it starts with you!

Culture within your organization starts with you and your leadership. You will set the tone and direction for the organization, and the values and behavior can have a significant influence on the culture of the organization. We have already discussed how you are also responsible for making decisions that shape the direction of the organization, but you also set the values and policies in pursuit of the values of the organization. Additionally, it is up to you to communicate the mission and values of your youth program to coaches, parents, and wrestlers, which can help to establish and maintain a strong organizational culture.

Once you have your culture established, your newer wrestlers will start to learn from your returning wrestlers, and then the cycle of passing the culture along will begin. Once it begins, a good culture is hard to break. Something to prioritize is the values you will build your culture around. These values need to be impactful, memorable, and easy to explain. Every wrestler in your program needs to be able to explain them at the end of their first season.

VALUES ARE A FOUNDATION

Your values are the foundation of your culture. If you have poor values, then you will have a poor culture. From my experience, I try to aim for five unique values. The values for my program are Respect, Integrity, Humility, Rise to the Occasion, and Have Fun While Being the Best. Each of those things is a part of the bigger picture of how I want them to grow as individuals. What are the things you want your wrestlers to be able to do that will set them apart from everyone else? We will talk about investing in their character in a later chapter, but for this section you need to determine what qualities you want your kids to be known for. Will they be known for their determination? Respect? How about discipline? Your choices here will set the direction for the growth of your athletes.

WRESTLERS ARE EACH OTHER'S BEST TEACHER

Over time, your kids who come back year over year will begin to know your expectations. The first few years it will be tough, and this is true for any major changes you will make to your program; however it will get easier as your retention rates increase! I've always said that kids are the best teachers of other kids. In the beginning, you will do most of the instruction, but on years two and three your experienced kids will be able to help make a lot of the adjustments for the new wrestlers. This can be technique or behavior expectations. For example, they take a knee instead of sitting on their bottoms. You may have to help teach them how to communicate appropriately, but it will allow for the teaching of more advanced concepts over time.

"Values are like fingerprints, nobody's are the same, but you leave them all over everything you do."
   - Elvis Presley

10.

AFFIRMATION

You know the goals, vision, mission, and values of your program, but do your wrestlers, parents, and the community? Developing well rounded wrestlers that come back starts with something simple. It is something that successful wrestling programs employ. It is an affirmation.

Affirmations play an important role in youth wrestling programs, especially new ones. They help boost the self-esteem, confidence, and motivation of young wrestlers. This is particularly beneficial for your younger wrestlers who may be just starting out in the sport and who may not yet have a solid understanding of their abilities and strengths. They typically internalize all of their struggles, losses, and frustrations. Affirmations help to counteract this negative self-talk. They provide young wrestlers with a positive and supportive message. When done daily, this can help to build resilience and even encourage young athletes to believe in themselves, even when facing challenges or setbacks. Your affirmation can even help them believe in you and what you are doing, which establishes a natural trust in what you're trying to accomplish.

Additionally, affirmations also help to reinforce the positive habits and behaviors that you are actively seeking to develop, such as staying focused, working hard, or being respectful, which are essential for success in wrestling and in life. Hearing and internalizing positive messages may result in young wrestlers being more likely to adopt those habits and behaviors and to achieve their goals. Want to see what I use in my program? Check out the **Roar of the Pride** before moving on.

Ridge Wrestling

ROAR OF THE PRIDE

WE ARE
LIONS
I AM
STRONG
SMART
I WILL
ATTACK
SCORE
HAVE FUN
WE ARE
PEACHTREE RIDGE
LIONS

At the end of the day, the use of affirmations can be a powerful tool for helping young wrestlers to develop a growth mindset, build resilience, and achieve success both in and out of the wrestling room. Let's look at a case study of a very successful program out of Alpharetta, Georgia.

Morris Fitness
WRESTLING

Prepare to be inspired by the incredible story of Coach Charlie Morris, the mastermind behind Morris Fitness in Alpharetta, Georgia. For over a decade, Coach Morris has been on a mission to build the ultimate wrestling program that not only produces champions but also cultivates a sense of community and self-belief. With an impressive record of over 25 kids sent to wrestle in college and an average of five to seven kids a year making that transition, Coach Morris has created a legacy of excellence that is hard to match.

What sets Coach Morris apart is his unwavering dedication to his program and his athletes. He is a coach who invests in his students from a young age, instilling in them the skills, discipline, and confidence needed to succeed both on and off the mat. Coach Morris is a firm believer in the power of positive affirmation, and every one of his athletes knows his affirmation statement by heart. It's this unwavering commitment to his athletes' growth and success that has made Morris Fitness a force to be reckoned with in the Georgia wrestling community.

If you're ready to take your youth wrestling program to the next level, then writing an affirmation is the proven approach you need. Check out the **MF Affirmation** for yourself and form your own opinion.

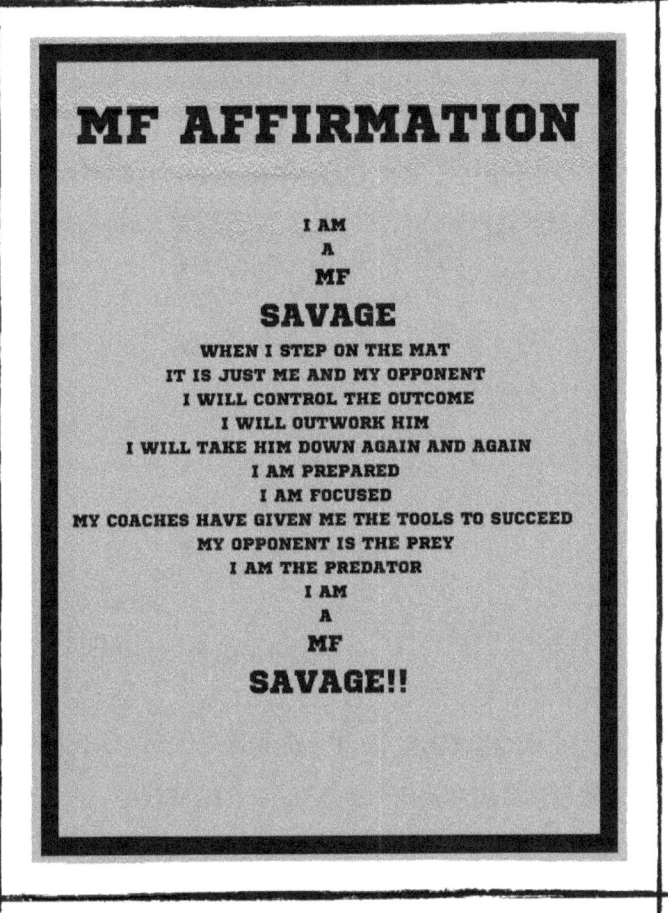

MF AFFIRMATION

I AM
A
MF
SAVAGE

WHEN I STEP ON THE MAT
IT IS JUST ME AND MY OPPONENT
I WILL CONTROL THE OUTCOME
I WILL OUTWORK HIM
I WILL TAKE HIM DOWN AGAIN AND AGAIN
I AM PREPARED
I AM FOCUSED
MY COACHES HAVE GIVEN ME THE TOOLS TO SUCCEED
MY OPPONENT IS THE PREY
I AM THE PREDATOR
I AM
A
MF
SAVAGE!!

CHALLENGE TIME

Building your affirmation starts and ends with what your kids are! Maybe you call your kids by their mascot or something cool like Luchadors. This identifier is going to be the core at which they build all other qualities around!

What will they be?

_____

_____

_____

_____

_____

The next several statements need to be memorable but have impact. If you only see your kids twice a week, it may be in your best interest to have shorter statements. If you'd see them more often, then it is easier to get them in step with something more wordy. Take the time to answer the questions below to help you craft your affirmation!

What are they? Establish the things they need to believe in!

_____

_____

_____

What are they doing?

_____

_____

_____

What is the objective?

_____

_____

_____

"I am the greatest, I said that even before I knew I was."
- Muhammad Ali

11.

SELL WRESTLING

Separating yourself and your program from other wrestling programs or even other sports is what differentiates building a wrestling program from building any other sport. In most areas, building a wrestling program means educating about wrestling and developing a plan to get the word out there.

The first step in selling your program is developing a plan to get the word out about what you are trying to do. It begins by targeting the local schools in the area. You'll want to get permission to put signs out and distribute flyers. Some may require you to get approval from their respective counties or school boards, so you'll want to jump on this early. Don't wait until the last minute to get this done or your turn out will not be what you expect. With your signs and flyers, you'll want to approach this with a single but specific strategy.

Signs

— Hardware: If you can shell out for the metal signs, then do it. You can use them year after year and they'll last. The cheaper plastic ones typically don't last as long and you won't be able to do as much with them.

— Design: Simple, unique, and colorful. It should have the title of your program. For example: 'Knights Youth Wrestling', the website where they can find you, 'KnightsYouthWrestling.com', and the mascot logo for your club.

— **Hot tip:** If you are a part of an association or organization that requires you to use their site for registration, then you can buy a domain and redirect it to their website. Your website needs to be easy to remember and easy to find. Odds are the parents will be in their cars when they see it. They shouldn't be using their phones when driving, and therefore they need to be able to remember it when they get to their destination.

— Quantity: I would look at putting one sign at every school for your boys AND girls side of your programs. Wrestling is generally Co-Ed, but if you want the girls to come then you need to advertise to them directly.

Flyers

— Design: These need to be the complete opposite of the signs. They need to have a picture of kids wrestling so parents can visualize the sport and then explain the sport of wrestling while being concise and straight to the point. No room for fancy or eloquent language here. This is a great opportunity to introduce potential wrestlers and their families to the sport of wrestling.

Questions you need to answer:

- Who should wrestle?

- Why should they wrestle?

- What is wrestling?

- Who is *Insert your club name here*?

- Is it easy?

- When is wrestling season?

- When are the practices?

- What is the cost?

- How do I sign up?

- Size: Make these half sheets printed in black and white to optimize on costs. If your local schools approve the flyers, then you can get them distributed in their 'Friday folders'.

ASSOCIATE A FACE WITH WRESTLING

You can distribute flyers and put up signs until you're blue in the face, but if you don't associate a face to what you're trying to build then you'll miss out on a lot of opportunity to bring in the families who are potentially willing to buy in. To put it simply, why would a family put their child into a sport that they know very little to nothing about? The answer is that you have to build a degree of trust. This means you have to get out to local events and talk to the kids and families directly. There are three ways you can do this and they all involve you!

Identify the fall sports in your area. You'll want to reach out to the directors and head coaches of the programs to set up times to talk to their teams. The traditional fall sports where you'll have the best response will most likely be football, soccer, and cheer. I would definitely reach out to the baseball and softball teams too, but with travel ball they're a much tougher sell and I would focus on the younger age groups. The whole goal is to talk to the kids and get them EXCITED about the sport of wrestling. That means talking about the things that they care about! Try to come up with something before hand that you can work with, a script if you will. Hit the points below in order.

- What is wrestling?

- Why will it make the better at the sport they are currently doing?

- How is wrestling fun?

- What are the fun things you'll do as a team?

Hot tip: Include a call to action and have them repeat this back to you. If they remember anything, you want them to go home and tell their parents that they want to wrestle!

Meet the parents where they are. That means going to their kids games and talking to them! Handing out flyers, educating parents, answering questions and overcoming objections. We will talk about the latter a little later, but the biggest part I want to touch on here is the initial conversation with the parent. Don't just walk up and spew your love for the sport. Take a moment to build some brief rapport. Ask them who they're at the event to watch! Give a genuine compliment about their kid or talk about something going on before jumping into wrestling. Some people are just going to be rude or flat out ignore you. Don't persist and just move on to someone who is willing to listen and talk. Your goal is to get them talking and be willing to have a conversation.

Hot tip: Avoid politics or anything that can be considered politics. My favorite topic to get people talking is the weather. They always have something to say about that!

Setup a table. Trust me on this. You may not get many people visiting your table, but the key here is visibility. The more they see you, the more they think about you. Some popular places to setup a table could be your local youth games, fairs, etc.

Hot Tip: Something that has been effective in the past was hosting a cookout and inviting families to join us. I used Social Media to get the word out and asked the local youth association to share it. I served over a hundred burgers and a hundred hot dogs at the event. It was a massive success!

Most people you talk to won't look at wrestling seriously. Some of the ways you can reach them is by talking about how wrestling will benefit them in other sports.

The honest truth is that skills and techniques developed in wrestling can be transferable to other sports and can help athletes improve their performance in their chosen sports. I break this down into six different domains. Wrestling can be beneficial to athletes of many sports in terms of developing balance and coordination, strength, mental toughness, reaction times and speed, flexibility and range of motion, and footwork.

Balance and coordination

Balance refers to the ability to maintain control over one's body in different positions and on different surfaces. Coordination refers to the ability to control one's movements effectively and efficiently. Wrestling requires a great deal of balance and coordination, as athletes need to move quickly, change direction, and maintain their balance during a match.
Example: A wrestler is able to maintain their balance while being taken down by

an opponent and then quickly counter-attacks to score.

Strength

Strength refers to the ability to exert force against an external resistance. Wrestling requires a lot of physical strength, as athletes need to be able to take down opponents, maintain control, and escape from holds.
Example: A wrestler who is able to lift and return their opponent to the mat, and then control them requires strength.

Mental toughness

Mental toughness refers to the ability to perform under pressure, push through fatigue and adversity, and maintain focus and concentration. Wrestling requires a lot of mental toughness, as athletes need to be able to perform at their best under stressful and challenging conditions.

Example: A wrestler who is able to stay focused and maintain their composure during a high-pressure match, even when they are tired or facing a tough opponent.

Reaction times and speed

Reaction time refers to the time it takes for an athlete to respond to a stimulus, such as an opponent's movement or a referee's call. Speed refers to how quickly an athlete can move. Wrestling requires a lot of quick reactions and movements, as athletes need to be able to anticipate and respond to their opponent's actions. Example: A wrestler is able to react quickly to an opponent's movement and then perform a quick takedown or escape from a hold.

Flexibility and range of motion

Flexibility refers to the ability of the joints and muscles to move through their full range of motion. Range of motion refers to the distance and direction in which a joint can move. Wrestling requires a lot of flexibility and range of motion, as athletes need to be able to move quickly and change direction, all while performing

different holds and maneuvers.
Example: A wrestler who is able to twist and turn their body to avoid an opponent's hold, and then quickly re-attacks with a hold of their own.

Footwork

Footwork refers to the movements of the feet and legs, and how they are used to maintain balance, move quickly, and change direction. Wrestling requires a lot of footwork, as athletes need to be able to move around the mat quickly and efficiently, while being able to perform different holds and takedowns at a moments notice.
Example: A wrestler who is able to move quickly and maintain their stance on the mat, and also use their footwork to move their opponent to set up a takedown or escape from a hold.

The good thing for you is that I have already put this list together for you. You can use this as your cheat sheet when preparing to talk to teams from other sports. You can thank me later.

Soccer

— Balance and coordination: Wrestling can help soccer players improve their balance and coordination on the field, especially with quick changes of direction, feints, and cuts.

— Strength: Wrestling can help soccer players develop their physical strength, which can be beneficial for winning battles for the ball and defending against opponents.

— Mental toughness: Wrestling can help soccer players develop their mental toughness, which can be beneficial for pushing through fatigue and adversity on the field.

— Reaction times and speed: Wrestling can help soccer players improve their reaction times and speed on the field, especially when it comes to quick movements and changes of direction.

— Flexibility and range of motion: Wrestling can help soccer players improve their flexibility and range of motion, which can be beneficial for quick movements and avoiding injuries.

— Footwork: Wrestling can help soccer players improve their footwork and agility on the field, especially when it comes to dodging defenders and making quick turns.

Football

— Balance and coordination: Wrestling can help football players improve their balance and coordination, which can be beneficial for maintaining balance and control during tackles and blocks.

— Strength: Wrestling can help football players develop their physical strength, which is crucial for making tackles and overpowering opponents.

— Mental toughness: Wrestling can help football players develop their mental toughness, which is crucial for pushing through fatigue and adversity on the field.

— Reaction times and speed: Wrestling can help football players improve their reaction times and speed on the field, which is crucial for making quick decisions and responding to opponents' movements.

— Flexibility and range of motion: Wrestling can help football players improve their flexibility and range of motion, which can be beneficial for quick movements and avoiding injuries.

— Footwork: Wrestling can help football players improve their footwork and agility, which is crucial for making quick cuts and changes of direction on the field.

Baseball

— Balance and coordination: Wrestling can help baseball players improve their balance and coordination, which can be beneficial for fielding and throwing.

– Strength: Wrestling can help baseball players develop their physical strength, which can be beneficial for hitting the ball harder and throwing with more velocity.

– Mental toughness: Wrestling can help baseball players develop their mental toughness, which is crucial for staying focused and performing under pressure.

– Reaction times and speed: Wrestling can help baseball players improve their reaction times and speed on the field, especially when it comes to fielding ground balls and catching fly balls.

– Flexibility and range of motion: Wrestling can help baseball players improve their flexibility and range of motion, especially pitchers who need to be able to rotate their shoulders and hips to generate power and speed on their pitches.

— Footwork: Wrestling can help baseball players improve their footwork and agility on the field, especially when it comes to turning double plays and fielding ground balls.

Lacrosse

— Balance and coordination: Wrestling can help lacrosse players improve their balance and coordination, which can be beneficial for maintaining control of the ball and dodging defenders.

— Strength: Wrestling can help lacrosse players develop their physical strength, which is crucial for winning battles for the ball and defending against opponents.

— Mental toughness: Wrestling can help lacrosse players develop their mental toughness, which is crucial for pushing through fatigue and adversity on the field.

— Reaction times and speed: Wrestling can help lacrosse players improve their reaction times and speed on the field, which is crucial for making quick decisions and responding to opponents' movements.

– Flexibility and range of motion: Wrestling can help lacrosse players improve their flexibility and range of motion, which is important for making quick movements and avoiding injuries.

– Footwork: Wrestling can help lacrosse players improve their footwork and agility on the field, especially when it comes to dodging defenders and making quick turns.

Cheerleading

– Balance and coordination: Wrestling can help cheerleaders improve their balance and coordination, which is crucial for performing stunts and tumbling.

– Strength: Wrestling can help cheerleaders develop their physical strength, which is crucial for performing stunts and lifts.

— Mental toughness: Wrestling can help cheerleaders develop their mental toughness, which is crucial for performing stunts and tumbling under pressure.

— Reaction times and speed: Wrestling can help cheerleaders improve their reaction times and speed, especially when it comes to performing stunts and tumbling.

— Flexibility and range of motion: Wrestling can help cheerleaders improve their flexibility and range of motion, which is crucial for performing stunts and tumbling.

— Footwork: Wrestling can help cheerleaders improve their footwork and agility, which is crucial for performing stunts and tumbling.

CLIMBING WALLS ISN'T EASY

Many times when you talk to people about their children wrestling you end up educating them about the sport. When people hear about wrestling, they typically have a couple of generic responses. Most of the time they think about organizations like WWE. Some may be already familiar with the sport but not for the right reasons like trash bags and starving. These preconceived notions result in them putting up the walls of objections. Developing a plan to educate those families means having discussions with them to overcome them. If you know what to expect, then you can prepare responses. Coming up in the Challenge Time section, you will be confronted with several of these challenges. It's better to formulate a response here than end up on the spot with no answers.

CHALLENGE TIME

It is time to put everything together and develop your plan.

My introduction to potential wrestlers when handing out flyers looks like...

_____

_____

_____

_____

_____

_____

Some places where I will hand out those flyers will be...

_____

_____

My introduction to families when handing out flyers looks like...

_____

_____

_____

_____

_____

_____

Some places where I will set up a table will be...

_____

_____

OVERCOMING OBJECTIONS

I am not going to lie to you. Some of these prompts are tough and may cover sensitive topics. These are real things that

I have heard from parents when discussing wrestling with them. You don't have to write a response, but if you have at least thought about it now, you won't be caught off by some of them like I was.

Wrestling is dangerous...

_____

_____

_____

_____

Wrestling causes eating disorders...

_____

_____

_____

_____

Wrestling just isn't for us. We are a football/baseball family...

_____

_____

_____

_____

Wrestling is too tough/rough for my son/daughter...

_____

_____

_____

_____

Wrestling is a 'gay' sport...

_____

_____

_____

_____

I don't want my son wrestling girls...

_____

_____

_____

_____

I don't want my daughter wrestling boys...

_____

_____

_____

_____

Wrestling is too much for my family...

_____

_____

_____

I don't want my child running in a trash bag...

_____

_____

_____

I don't want to spend all day in a gym...

_____

_____

_____

The rules are too confusing...

_____

_____

_____

An objection is not a rejection. It is a simple request for more information.
-Bo Bennett

12.

BUILDING A GIRLS PROGRAM

Building an independent girls program is arguably just as important as the main program in general. I strongly believe that building girls programs increases the impact wrestling has on communities, and it starts with a simple phrase. "If you build it, they will come." I said this to myself over and over as I battled rejection after rejection for girls wrestling in my community. The truth is that girls wrestling is growing faster than boys wrestling right now, and if you want to grow your program quickly, being able to cater to both is important.

First, I need to address the elephant in the room: building a girls program doesn't mean you're going to have to sacrifice anything in your program or from the boys program. Girls have many of the same needs as boys and the program requires very small changes to the way you as a director/head coach will operate it. If anything, the additional registrations will bring in additional revenue that you can use for everyone!

IF YOU BUILD IT

When it comes to building girls wrestling programs, I have always said a twist on a popular phrase, "If you build it, they will come." The original phrase came from the movie *Field of Dreams* where the protagonist Ray Kinsella goes out on a limb to build a field with the hope that *the* "Shoeless Joe Jackson" will come to his field. He toiled and toiled, facing bankruptcy and adversity, but he eventually achieved his goal. When building your program, know that there is light at the end of the tunnel, it just takes time.

Recruiting girl wrestlers starts with getting other girls to buy into wrestling. As the girls team grows, there will be more girls that are interested in wrestling. It is important to encourage the girls on the team to be ambassadors for the sport. They are the ones who can talk to their friends and convince them to come out and try the sport.

When girls see other girls on the mat, they are more likely to be interested in trying it out for themselves. It is important to empower the girls on the team to share their experiences and to show other girls that wrestling is a sport that is for them. Girls tend to bond over shared experiences and interests, so it is important to create a welcoming environment where they feel comfortable talking to their friends about wrestling.

As the girls team grows, it is important to continue to foster a sense of community among the girl wrestlers. Encourage them to support each other and to be there for each other both on and off the mat. When girls feel like they are part of a community, they are more likely to stick with the sport and to recruit other girls to join them.

In addition, it is important to showcase the girls team and their accomplishments. Share photos and videos on social media and on your team's website. This will help to promote the girls team and show other girls that they too can be successful in the sport.

WRESTLING IS FOR THEM

Building a girls program starts by making the girls feel like wrestling is for them! When you distribute flyers in a school, flyers specifically for girls showcasing girls wrestling. When you make signs to advertise, you need to have signs that feature a female wrestler. Ultimately you have to reach them where **they are**. You have to pitch wrestling as a sport **for them**! They have to **feel** like it is something that they can see themselves doing. Remember that wrestling is a male dominated sport and odds are they do not personally know any females in the sport. You're going to have to build the rapport of the sport for them since they most likely have no knowledge of the sport.

Most objections you will receive for girls wrestling will come from the parents. We talked a little bit in a previous chapter about overcoming objections, and for girls it will be very similar, with different objections. The biggest objections I receive tend to be from dads concerned about their daughters wrestling boys. A lot of times this is absolved once their daughters are practicing in a room. Once they see it is something that their daughters can do many of their concerns will resolve on their own. I've had success referring to the opportunities available in the area and the rapidly growing aspect of the sport.

The second largest objection I receive tends to be about the uniform. Speaking honestly, explaining the difference between a mens and women's singlet is like talking to a wall. Offering a two-piece option and then explaining the differences between the uniforms is your best bet. One of our program sponsors, www.SnapdownDesigns.com, sews mini bralettes into our singlets for the girls who order one, but the standard uniform for our team is a two piece. Remember it is not the singlet that is the problem. It is about how the girls feel about how they look.

ORGANIZING PRACTICE

As a wrestling coach, it's important to consider the best approach when it comes to girls wrestling during practice. There are different schools of thought out there, but ultimately, the goal should be to create an inclusive and supportive environment for all athletes.

Personally, I prefer to practice my boys and girls teams in the same room, teaching coed while keeping them separated for drilling. This approach allows me to keep both groups engaged and focused during practice. It also allows me to release one group if they have grasped the techniques, while retaining the other to answer questions or expand on what I am showing.

While some girls may end up partnering with boys based on need and parent approval, the ultimate goal is to keep everyone together. Wrestling in a coed environment can be a positive experience, as it provides opportunities for athletes to learn from and challenge each other. It can also help create a more inclusive and diverse wrestling community.

However, as your program grows, you may find that having separate practices for boys and girls is necessary. If this is the case, I would suggest waiting until you have enough athletes to justify the additional practice time. Separating your girls team if there are only a few members may not be the best approach, as it can lead to isolation and a lack of opportunity to learn from a diverse group of wrestlers.

At the end of the day, the most important thing is to create a positive and supportive environment for all wrestlers, regardless of gender. Whether you choose to practice coed or have separate practices for boys and girls, it's essential to foster a sense of community, respect, and inclusivity within your wrestling program.

"A girl can do anything she wants to do, and nobody can tell her she can't."
- Shirley Chisholm

13.

CHOOSING YOUR CURRICULUM

Crafting a curriculum is more than just saying *"I am going to teach this stuff"*. It is an evolving art. You have to learn how to adapt to challenge and change based on the environment around you. Your population will determine a lot of it, but that's not the only thing you'll need to worry about.

When I said that your curriculum needs to always evolve, I meant it. You'll start with fundamentals and then work your way into the more difficult technique. The important thing is making sure the CORE of your curriculum is the same now, and in five years. Whatever you choose, you don't want to pick something and then do a dramatic change in two years. You'd basically be starting over if you did. My suggestions for the core of your curriculum breaks down into several questions.

What will be your first takedown?

My suggestion is to not make this complicated. It should be fast and easy to teach and learn. Some examples of fast and easy moves are double legs, snapdown go-behinds, and headlocks.

What will be your second more complicated takedown?

This is a great space for high scoring moves like single legs, hi-crotches, Russian (2 on 1) ties, and underhooks.

What will be your first breakdown?

There are five main options here. Chop and boot, spiral rides, double knee block, thigh pries, and tight waist far ankle. The latter is the easiest to teach, but can be the most difficult for kids to transition from. Either way, you want to make sure you teach your kids how to **ride** their opponents and not just get them flat.

What will be your first pinning combination?

Depending on your age groups, you may want to choose to do something different. A tried and true pinning combination that is very successful on all levels is a basic half. Unless you have a good reason to do something different, I'd make sure this is on your list.

How will your kids get off bottom?

Getting off bottom is crucial to long-term success. Matches can be decided by as little as a point. The fastest way off bottom for a new wrestler though is a standup. There are several different ways to teach it, but whatever you do be consistent.

Your curriculum is going to change, especially as you start to layer your teaching. In subsequent seasons, you'll want to tie in additional and more advanced technique! The important thing is that you are tying into things your returning kids already know. Your program's culture will help fill in the gaps.

Something else to keep in mind is how much you teach. I scale my teaching based on the age group. Ultimately, they only have to be **great** at two or three moves to win some big events like State. The kicker is that not all kids are going to be great at the same thing. You also have to keep the age group in mind as some things are more appropriate than others. A green five year old isn't going to be ready for moves like Russian ties or throws, but they could be great at a snap down go behind or a double leg. I've listed some examples below so you can get an idea of the progression.

6 and Under - Little Kids

Takedown: Snap down go behind, Double Leg
Breakdown: Tight waist far ankle
Pinning combo: Half and wrist
Scoring on bottom: Stand up

8 and Under, 10 and Under - Elementary

Takedown: Snap down go behind, double leg, single leg
Breakdown: Tight waist far ankle, chop and boot
Pinning combo: Half and wrist, bar and half
Scoring on bottom: Stand up, switch

12 and Under, 14 and Under - Middle School

Takedown: Snap down go behind, double leg, single leg, Russian/underhook ties
Breakdown: Tight waist far ankle, chop and boot, spiral ride
Pinning combo: Half and wrist, bar and half, cradles
Scoring on bottom: Stand up, switch, granby roll

CHALLENGE TIME

It is time to write down the core of your curriculum. This isn't concrete, but will be a good place to go back to when you are trying to lay down the 2nd and 3rd layers of your curriculum during the 2nd and 3rd years of your program. On the next page, you'll fill in your core curriculum. Follow the P's when planning and you'll have great success.

Proper Preparation & Planning

Prevents Poor Performance

There's plenty of space to write, so feel free to use it as a white board. It is broken up by age groups, so be sure to think about your progression here. You may not jump into all of it your first year, but you need to have a plan!

My Core Curriculum

1st Takedown:

2nd Takedown:

1st Breakdown:

1st Pinning Combination:

1st Bottom Move:

My 8U and 10U Core Curriculum

1st Takedown:

2nd Takedown:

3rd Takedown:

_____

_____

1st Breakdown:

_____

_____

2nd Breakdown:

_____

_____

1st Pinning Combination:

_____

_____

2nd Pinning Combination:

_____

_____

1st Bottom Move:

_____

_____

2nd Bottom Move:

_____

_____

My 12U and 14U Core Curriculum

1st Takedown:

_____

_____

2nd Takedown:

_____

_____

3rd Takedown:

_____

_____

4th Takedown or Control Ties:

_____

_____

1st Breakdown:

_____

_____

2nd Breakdown:

_____

_____

3rd Breakdown:

_____

_____

1st Pinning Combination:

_____

_____

2nd Pinning Combination:

_____

3rd Pinning Combination:

1st Bottom Move:

2nd Bottom Move:

3rd Bottom Move:

"We are what we repeatedly do. Excellence, then, is not an act, but a habit."
  - Aristotle

14.

BUILDING A WINNING TEAM

Recruiting a dedicated and skilled board of directors and coaching staff is crucial for the success of any youth wrestling program. Not only does it demonstrate to parents and participants that the program is serious and committed to excellence, but it also provides critical support for managing the day-to-day operations of the program. However, finding the right people to fill these roles can be a challenge. In this chapter, we'll discuss strategies for building a strong and effective board of directors, including the roles and responsibilities of each position. We'll also explore how to recruit and train coaches, as well as how to build a positive and cohesive team culture that supports the growth and development of all participants.

Once your youth wrestling program grows to over 10-15 kids, recruiting a board and coaching staff becomes critical to the program's success. A full board is essential for long-term success, as is having an adequate number of coaches. Ideally, there should be one coach for every four to five kids, regardless of gender. For example, a program of 40 kids would require a minimum of eight coaches, not counting yourself; however, finding and convincing individuals to volunteer their time and knowledge and align with your program's mission can be challenging.

WELCOME

I would recommended that at the beginning of each season, a parent meeting be held within the first four weeks. This is an opportunity to not only introduce your program, but also to provide a broad overview of expectations and introduce leadership. As this may be the first experience with the sport of wrestling for many families, it is important to maintain a professional, friendly, and positive demeanor. This initial interaction sets the tone for building the foundation of new relationships.

FAMILIES BEGIN WITH RELATIONSHIPS

Establishing a wrestling family and community begins with forging connections with individuals. Often, the first families to enroll in your wrestling program will have prior experience in wrestling or other martial arts, while others may be seeking an outlet for their high-energy kids. Cultivating a relationship with these families should be a top priority. Once you have established a rapport and gained an understanding of their backgrounds, you can delve into their motivations for trying wrestling. Armed with this knowledge, you can make a compelling appeal to them.

ASK FOR HELP

It's common for some people to feel hesitant about asking for help. When I first started out, I also struggled with this feeling. Even when people offered to assist, I still tried to handle everything on my own, but eventually realized the importance of seeking help. This step is crucial because in order to grow your program, you'll need to surround yourself with individuals you can empower. Before even considering coaches, it's essential to establish a Board and fill several key positions. The sooner you do this, the sooner you can shift your focus to important matters that affect the program as a whole. I've outlined the positions and their potential responsibilities below, although they can be tailored to meet your individual needs rather than strictly following my definition.

Necessary Board Positions

— **President/Chair/Director -** This is the key leader for the youth board. They are responsible for running meetings, organizing, and providing necessary leadership oversight. They create the agenda for meetings. This individual is able to delegate responsibilities to other officers or club representatives as needed or desired. The position is the primary contact for the board and is in consistent communication with other clubs, wrestling organization leaders, and other invested parties.

They are instrumental in creating a vision and mission for the future. They should be dedicated and passionate about wrestling and are likely to be in attendance at most if not a good number of regional activities over the course of the year. This individual seeks out and creates partnerships and opportunities for the program and the youth board. This individual is ultimately responsible for the success or failure of a program.

— **Vice President/Vice Chair/Assistant Director** - This individual acts as a backup for the President/Chair/Director. They are responsible for assisting in anything the President/Chair/Director needs help with. In the case that the President/Chair/Director is unable to attend a meeting or coordinate something, this individual should step in. This position is a good way to prepare someone to be President/Chair/Director. They communicate frequently with the other youth board members to be sure tasks are completed on time.

— **Secretary** - This person takes meeting minutes that should be made available to the representatives within a few days. They are instrumental in keeping documents organized on a platform such as OneDrive, Google Drive, or OpenDrive. Depending on the exact setup of the board, they may send emails to members or representatives at the request of the President/Chair/Director. This person ensures documentation (ex. electronic or paper hardcopies) is organized and all paperwork is done correctly and on time.

— **Treasurer** - This position is responsible for ensuring that budgets are created and balanced. They are also in charge of managing the board finances. In addition to creating budgets, they should collect and deposit payments from events or fundraisers, and write checks when necessary. This individual must be 18 years old since they will need to be able to access the club bank account and fully function in the position. The Treasurer should not hold a chair or vice chair position due to conflict of interest in handling the finances.

Optional Additional Positions

— **Fundraising Chair -** This individual is the first optional position that I would suggest. If your program does a lot of fundraising, then this should be sought with urgency. This individual takes any fundraisers that have been voted on by the board and organizes them. They typically work hand in hand with the Treasurer when it comes to getting funds deposited.

— **Website Manager/Social Media Chair -** This position is important if you have an online website or social media presence. They would be responsible for managing the website and in charge of creating and/or collecting content and consistently posting to Social Media outlets (Facebook, Instagram, TikTok, etc.). They should have access to all photos and videos taken by the club.

— **High School Liaison -** This position is important if your club will function as a part of or in conjunction with a high school wrestling program. Assuming that your youth program will have its own meetings, this individual will be responsible for attending the meetings for the Youth and High School boards. They should advocate for the youth program interests when attending the High School Board meetings and relay any important or critical information to the youth board.

— **Volunteer Coordinator -** This position is important if you host a lot of events. This individual would be responsible for managing and coordinating volunteers for all home events. Additionally, if you do community service events then they could help coordinate the event.

Non Board Positions

Coaches

Good wrestling programs are organized with a diverse coaching staff, consisting of Head Coaches, Assistant Coaches, and Junior Coaches, each playing a crucial role in the development of their athletes. Each coaching position serves a unique purpose, from managing practices and curriculum to providing support and fostering a culture of giving back to the community.

– **Head Coaches** - This is a tough one because wrestling is not structured like other sports. The goal is to eventually have a head coach for each age group; however, when you are starting small, it may be best to group them together. In my program I grouped them by Elementary, Middle and Girls teams. As the groups grew, I divided them as necessary. This position is responsible for running practices, implementing the curriculum, and communicating the needs of their team to the Board.

— **Assistant Coaches** - These positions are held by parents or individuals who want to be involved in wrestling but do not have the experience or expertise to be a Head Coach. They can be floating coaches or be assigned to assist a specific Head Coach. These positions should only be held by adults 18+.

— **Junior Coaches** - This position is a great way to let high school wrestlers contribute to your youth program without having to give them serious responsibilities. If you foster a culture of giving back, then as your eighth graders move to high school they will come back to work with the program.

Support

The best wrestling programs thrive on the support from dedicated individuals in various roles, such as Manager Coordinators, Managers, Team Moms, and Photographers. These roles contribute to the smooth functioning of the program by managing tasks ranging from recruitment and coordination to capturing memorable moments and fostering team spirit.

- **Manager Coordinator -** This individual is responsible for recruiting and managing the team managers. They should coordinate with the head coaches about needs and scheduling.

- **Managers -** These positions are typically held by Middle School or High School students who aren't old enough to hold serious responsibilities but are old enough to be responsible for a few tasks such as keeping score, recording film, or collecting uniforms.

— **Team Mom -** This individual or group of individuals would be responsible for putting together the chow box of snacks, communicating important team information, and working with the Board to coordinate the banquet.

— **Photographer -** This individual should be responsible for taking pictures at all events. They should coordinate with the Secretary to get the pictures saved and made available to the Website Manager / Social Media Chair.

APPRECIATE

It's important to not only recruit people to join your program but also to retain them year over year. One way to achieve this is by showing appreciation for their contributions. This can be done in various ways, and it's essential to take advantage of every opportunity to do so.

For example: there are two major holidays during the folkstyle wrestling season that can be used to show gratitude. You can give a gift or send them a personal message of gratitude. However, appreciation is more than just saying thank you; it starts with valuing their opinions and addressing them in a respectful and meaningful manner.

It's important to make every member, even high schoolers, feel valued and included. After all, they are part of the family, and you want them to feel like they never left even after they graduate. Remember that appreciation doesn't stop at the individual member but also extends to their families.

It's essential to recognize that their participation could be reliant on the approval of their spouse, and their support is also vital to the success of the program. By making everyone feel like they are an integral part of the program, you can foster a sense of loyalty and commitment that will keep them coming back year after year.

When it comes to building your coaching staff and board, it's important to look for people who share your vision and passion for wrestling. You want to find people who are willing to put in the time and effort to help the program succeed.

When recruiting coaches, look for individuals who have experience and knowledge of the sport, as well as strong communication and leadership skills. You want coaches who can connect with the athletes and help them to develop their skills and confidence.

For your board, seek out individuals who can bring diverse perspectives and skill sets to the table. Look for people with expertise in areas such as finance, marketing, and community outreach. A strong board can help you to raise funds, build partnerships, and increase visibility for your program.

Ultimately, building a strong coaching staff and board requires time, effort, and a commitment to excellence. By valuing the contributions of everyone involved and recruiting individuals who share your passion and vision, you can create a program that is successful both on and off the mat.

THE FORMULA WORKS

The four-step approach (Welcome, Families, Ask for Help, Appreciate) outlined in this chapter may seem familiar to those with experience in youth athletics or sales, as it is a proven formula used and taught in various industries. Successful salespeople consistently adhere to these principles, which can also be observed in popular retail settings, such as Best Buy, where it serves as an essential component of their sales training program.

Just as in sales, establishing a thriving wrestling program involves winning over stakeholders and securing their commitment. By effectively implementing and replicating these four steps, you can enhance your program's retention rates, fostering a stronger sense of community and ultimately achieving your objectives.

"Surround yourself with the best people you can find, delegate authority, and don't interfere."
- President Ronald Reagan

15.

SAFETY PLAN

Safety is as important as you make it and having a plan is important. Don't skim over this section. It starts with being able to prepare your kids for wrestling, teach them proper hygiene practices, teach them the rules, and how to be aware of their surroundings. Then we will get into the emergency plan and what your steps should be during an incident. Your safety plan is how you will prevent, prepare for, and respond to potential safety events.

Preparation is key to the success of anything we do. Well, you already know that since you're reading this. Imprinting the success plan to ensure the safety of your wrestlers onto your parents is the first step. What does this look like? It's simple. Create an equipment checklist.

You'll want to include things like headgear, shoes, and mouth pieces.

Hot tip: *If there is a specific type of head gear or shoes that you don't wan't your kids wearing, list it as a no-no!*

Additionally, include the do's and don'ts for gear. For my practice rooms I have no zippers and pockets rule and this is included on my equipment checklist. The bottom line is I want my parents to know up front what they can do to make sure their child is safe.

HYGIENE IS A REAL ISSUE

Skin infections are a common problem in wrestling and most people hear about the worst cases. Ringworm, impetigo herpes, staph, and even MSRA are all risks in your room. It is important to have a cleaning schedule for daily and annual sanitation. If you're using the traditional heavy mats, then I would suggest flipping your mats and cleaning both sides and the floor underneath every year if not at least every two years. You don't want anything festering beneath your mats. For the daily cleaning sessions, you want to have it cleaned before practice. If your youth practice is following your high school practice, clean between the sessions. When it comes to your solution you can mix it yourself with bleach and water or use premixed solutions from Dollamur or KenClean. If you ever have an infection break out, then you can refer to your safety plan for what to do next.

SAFETY PLANS NEED TO INCLUDE A RESPONSE

One of the most important aspects of running a youth wrestling program is ensuring the safety and well-being of your athletes. In the event that one of your kids is hurt, you need to have a plan in place to respond quickly and effectively. This includes having emergency contact information readily available to your coaches so that they can call 911 and emergency contacts if necessary. It's also important to consider where an ambulance would park and the fastest way to get to where you practice, in case they need to be called. While it may be a rare occurrence, being prepared and having this information readily available can make all the difference in the event of an emergency.

Another important aspect of responding to injuries is having medical supplies readily available in your wrestling room. While a school or facility may have a trainer who can assist with injuries, it's important to have a basic medkit on hand to handle minor injuries like nosebleeds or cuts. A medkit should include items like bandages, nose plugs, medical tape, prewrap, antibiotic ointment, gloves, flex wrap, alcohol wipes, and Vaseline. If you or your coaching staff need training in First Aid, there are many resources available. Organizations like AmericanBLS.com offer a free basic First Aid course, while many state sport governing bodies offer more in-depth or hands-on training. By being prepared and having the necessary supplies and training in place, you can help ensure the safety and well-being of your athletes, and be ready to respond quickly and effectively in the event of an injury.

PREVENTING INJURY ESCALATIONS

Safety during practice starts with how you implement live wrestling, drilling, and teaching. If you haven't ran a wrestling program, or have limited experience with wrestling, then you're going to need to go a step further than most people who have the experience. Proper spacing, appropriate points for safety when teaching the sport is important. The American Sport Education Program has a great book titled 'Coaching Youth Wrestling' that goes into a lot of this. It is worth digging into if you have limited experience in the sport.

"Safety does not happen by accident."
- Unknown

16.

INVEST IN THEIR CHARACTER

Wrestling isn't like other sports. Football players call themselves football players. People who choose to wrestle call themselves wrestlers. Developing a program that values the wrestlers as people and not just as athletes is critical to the long-term success of your program. Coaching is already a complex and multifaceted profession that requires a wide range of skills and expertise. Developing this identity and, ultimately, champions both on and off the mat is the ability to help wrestlers grow not only their physical skills, but also their character. This includes values-based learning, both inside and outside of the wrestling room.

BE POSITIVE

One way coaches can invest in the character of their wrestlers is by creating and maintaining a positive and supportive culture in the wrestling room. This includes setting clear expectations and rules, recognizing and rewarding good behavior, and holding athletes accountable for their actions. Coaches should model the good behavior they expect and should be consistent in their expectations and responses to athletes.

INCORPORATE YOUR VALUES

Incorporating values-based learning into the training process is another way coaches can invest in the character of their wrestlers. This can involve teaching wrestlers about the importance of teamwork, sportsmanship, respect, and the other core program values. This process is important in wrestling and in life. We use lesson plans that typically happen at the beginning of practice. Some may be structured, while others came from devotionals. You'll be developing your own plans for the most part, but make sure that you give the kids a chance to chime in.

Something that I found to make a real impact outside of the wrestling room was the use of poker chips. Pete Jacobson from WinSmarter.com gave me this idea, and it was a huge success. When we handed them out, we told the kids to take them everywhere they went because it was a reminder of what it meant to be a Peachtree Ridge wrestler. I told them to show their teachers because we wanted them to know that we were supporting them. When the kids didn't do what they should have been doing, their parents sent them back to the coaches to turn in their poker chip. Just the response from the parents alone was overwhelming. I had always told them that we want to support them in and outside of the practice room, but when they saw this I believe that they really believed me! The kids loved them, and the truth is the poker chips meant something to them. After a talk with the coach and a good practice to earn it back, we had no repeat offenders.

DEVELOP THEM INSIDE AND OUTSIDE OF THE WRESTLING ROOM

You can develop your kids outside of the wrestling room too. You can invest in the character of your wrestlers by providing opportunities for service and leadership. This can involve organizing community service projects or encouraging wrestlers to take on leadership roles within the team, their schools, or communities. We worked with a local nursing home to put on a 'game day' where we invited the residents to participate. They were paired off with the kids while some served drinks and snacks. By participating in these activities, wrestlers can develop valuable skills and a sense of purpose and responsibility. Did I mention that parents love to see this kind of activities? THEY LOVE THEM!

OPPORTUNITIES FOR GROWTH

Another way you and your coaches can invest in the character of your wrestlers is by providing opportunities for personal and professional growth. This can involve individually helping wrestlers identify and pursue their interests and passions, encouraging them to take on new challenges and responsibilities, and providing support and resources for their growth and development. This also means talking to them about goal setting. Some families may look toward you as their child's coach to help their children learn things like responsibility. It's not what most coaches expect, but it is what will make your athletes successful.

BE AVAILABLE

Finally, coaches can invest in the character of their wrestlers by being open, transparent, and approachable. This can involve being available to listen and support wrestlers, being honest and upfront about expectations, and being open to feedback and suggestions. By being open and approachable, coaches can help wrestlers feel valued and supported, which can in turn help to build trust and strengthen relationships.

"Your wrestlers will ultimately reflect what type of energy and effort you put in. If you put in the excellence you expect, then they will display excellence in their every day lives."
- Tre Horton

17.

PLANNING YOUR PRACTICES

Preparation leads to success not just in life but in wrestling as well. If you are a painter and all you do every day you paint is throw paint at the wall, then there's no way you're going to finish a mural. Practice planning is what takes paint and turns it into art. It's more than just knowing what you're going to do everyday. Practice planning is about the journey from where you start the day and where you want to end up. It's meant to give you a road plan to satisfy the daily goal you have for the day. Practice planning is about setting your program up for success because practices are intentional. Every practice plan has five main components: the meeting, the warm up, the lesson, the cardio and games, and the wrestling.

PROPER PREPARATION LEADS TO SUCCESS

Every practice should begin with a meeting of some kind. This is your opportunity to set expectations for the practice, teach a lesson, or review film. Setting expectations is the easiest way to set yourself and your wrestlers up to meet goals every day.

GETTING READY TO WRESTLE

Warm ups are important. When done properly, they can build stamina and prevent injury during practice. The important thing is that your warm up is designed for the kids to break a sweat and prepare their bodies for wrestling. What does a good warm up look like? For

K-8 programs, this is a great time to do some running, calisthenics, and tumbling. They are still trying to learn their bodies and position in space and these exercises that in the beginning will be tough, but ultimately pay off.

When you get to your stretching, I would STRONGLY urge you to look up dynamic stretching. It is a great way to prevent injury and the benefits are undeniable. If you are familiar with static stretching (touch your toes and hold it for 30 seconds) then dynamic stretching is taking the same stretching goals and incorporating movement. The Cleveland Clinic has a great article on the differences between the two forms of stretching. Dr. Anne Rex from the article explains it like this "Dynamic stretching mimics the activity or the movement that you're going to do in whatever sport or activity you're about to start". If you're looking for a great way to improve performance and prevent injury, then dynamic stretching is what you're going to want to do.

TEACHING ISN'T EASY

Teaching is not easy. I am going to say it again. Teaching is not easy. Something that will make it easier is linking what you teach from practice to practice. What I am saying is, if I teach a double leg on Monday, then a Hi-Crotch would be a great thing to teach on a Tuesday because it reuses a lot of the same movements and can reinforce what was taught on Monday. Finding ways to link techniques builds links between things the kids learn. The more technical links you build the more likely they are to remember and be able to perform.

CARDIO IS KEY

Cardio is important in wrestling, but It is even more important to make sure your kids have fun. If done right, your games can act as your cardio. USA Wrestling has great resources for a list and description of games. Your biggest resource though are going to be neighboring clubs. Calling up their coaches and asking them what games do and don't work for them are a great way to get started. The biggest thing you can do though is make competition out of your normal drills. An example of this is the toe touch game. The goal is to touch the toes of your opponent without diving, standing up, and staying on your feet. It emphasizes the ability to level change, take shots, sprawling, and moving in your stance. All beneficial for wrestling and the kids don't realize the good muscle memory they are building.

COMPETITIVE WRESTLING NEEDS TO HAPPEN IN THE ROOM

Live wrestling is important for practice. Time can be limited some times with the pacing of practice, but I try to do this at least once a week. This gives the kids a chance to put what they learn to practice. If you're in a larger room, it makes sense to break the kids up into two groups based on age or weight. If you're in a smaller room, you can group them into groups of three or four.

The important thing is keeping the sessions short and keeping the kids spaced out far enough that they can't land on each other. They need to learn the competitive attitude and how to compete in the practice room before their first match. This is a great time to employ your coaching staff to walk around and keep an eye on kids. A rule of thumb is that if it looks like a dangerous position to be in, stop the wrestling and reset them.

A lot of kids don't know when to stop and will keep going even in the face of danger. Why? Because in the heat of the moment, they don't know what it should and shouldn't feel like. Remember, they are still learning their position in space so your ability to access when and where what they are doing is too dangerous.

If you want your program to be successful, then you have to have a plan for every time you step into your room. I've put together practice plans for you on my website. Swing by www.BuildYourYouthProgram.com to pickup your free wrestling practice plan template. Use it. Stay organized.

"Preparation is key in the world of wrestling. It's not just about showing up on the day of the match and hoping for the best. It's about putting in the time and effort to train, to strategize, and to fine-tune every aspect of your game. When you're prepared, you're confident. And when you're confident, you can take on anyone."
- Tre Horton

18.

FUN IS MORE THAN JUST A WORD

I talked a little bit already about games during practice with your practice plan, but fun is more than just games. Wrestling is already such a physically and mentally demanding sport that requires a high level of dedication and discipline. While the focus of wrestling practices is typically on improving technique and building conditioning, it is equally important for you and your coaches to incorporate fun into your training sessions.

Fun needs to be a key component to have a successful wrestling program. It may determine if the wrestlers come back! In my experience, it is the number one reason why kids choose to come back or not, at ALL levels. If you are going to be focused on retention, then you don't want to let this fall through the cracks.

INCORPORATE THE FUN

Incorporating fun into wrestling practices can have a number of benefits for both coaches and athletes. For one, it can help to create a positive and enjoyable team culture, which if you read the chapter on building your culture, you know how important this is. It can foster a sense of camaraderie and encourage athletes to stay committed to the sport. When practices are enjoyable, wrestlers are more motivated to attend and work hard and give their best effort, which can lead to better performance and skill development.

In addition to improving the team dynamics, incorporating fun into wrestling practices can also help to break up the monotony of training and keep athletes motivated and engaged. This can be especially important for wrestlers who may be dealing with a lot of stress at home or just the physical and mental challenges of the sport. When practices are enjoyable, your wrestlers are more likely to stay engaged, which can help them to perform better and ultimately learn more.

There are a number of ways that you and your coaches can incorporate fun into wrestling practices. An easy approach is to mix up the daily routine by introducing new drills or activities that challenge them in different ways. This can help to keep practices fresh and engaging, and depending on what you do can also help to develop new skills.

Another way to make practices more enjoyable is to allow for some free time for wrestlers to drill the moves of their choosing or plan some dedicated time for games. Allowing wrestlers to choose their own drills or play games during practice creates a more relaxed and informal atmosphere, which can help athletes feel more comfortable and engaged. It gives the kids a chance to explore the moves they have learned and can give them the opportunity to bond and build relationships with their teammates. If wanted to mix both together, you could have skill based games that to the kids are games but also teach them a specific skill.

ATMOSPHERE MATTERS

Positive reinforcement and encouragement are powerful tools for coaches to create a fun and positive atmosphere during practices. Instead of solely focusing on criticism, consequences, or punishment, coaches should prioritize reinforcing positive behavior. When athletes feel supported and valued, they are more likely to be motivated and engaged in practices, and their performance can improve.

Coaches can provide positive reinforcement in a variety of ways. For example, coaches can praise athletes for their effort, attitude, and progress, or provide specific feedback that recognizes their hard work and achievements. Coaches can also create a sense of accomplishment by celebrating the team's successes, such as individual or team wins, and recognizing individual milestones.

Using positive reinforcement and encouragement is effective because it helps to build a positive team culture, fosters a sense of camaraderie, and keeps athletes motivated and engaged in their training. Instead of creating a negative or punitive atmosphere, which can lead to disengagement or resentment, positive reinforcement helps to build trust and respect between the coach and athletes. When coaches focus on positive behavior, they are more likely to create an environment in which athletes feel safe, comfortable, and supported, which can help them to perform at their best.

TEAM BUILDING IS IMPORTANT

Everyone knows that wrestling is an individual sport. By creating a strong team culture through activities like team building events, coaches can help retain athletes year over year. This means taking the thing that other sports do best and bringing it to wrestling and ultimately your program.

Everything you do matters and your values are reflected in what type of activities you are doing. A popular activity for my youth wrestling teams has been taking them to watch a local college wrestling team. It was a great opportunity for them to experience high level wrestling and to get excited about the sport. If you don't have a college team near by, you can accomplish something similar to this by attending a local high school dual. Most coaches would love the opportunity to increase the size of their home crowd. They may even let your team in for free if you ask! Don't pass up the opportunity to reinforce note taking while you're there.

Hot Tip: Tell your kids to bring sharpies and get there early to have a chance to get shirts signed!

SMILING IS JUST AS IMPORTANT

Losing can be tough, and for kids, it can be especially hard. As a coach, it's important to remember that the goal of youth sports is not just about winning, but also about teaching kids important life skills and values. One of those values is resilience, and helping kids bounce back from a loss with a positive attitude is crucial in developing that skill.

One way to do that is by making them laugh or smile after a loss. This doesn't mean making light of the situation or disregarding the loss, but rather finding ways to help the kids see the positive aspects of the experience. By creating a lighthearted moment or bringing some humor into the situation, you can help shift the focus from the negative emotions associated with losing to a more positive outlook. This can help kids feel more comfortable with taking risks and trying new things, which is important for their growth and development both on and off the mat. It can also help build a stronger bond between the coach and the athletes, which can lead to more trust and a deeper level of respect.

Meet Lionel. When I had him made I took a leap of faith. Simply put, my goal was to have something to bring down all off the walls kids put up after they lose. They're out there, alone with no one else to blame for losing but themselves. Most will internalize this loss negatively. Many kids who are new to the sport struggle with their emotions, and to be a successful coach you have to learn how to be their partner in that process.

In the end, Lionel's presence on the team has been an incredible addition. After every loss, he is brought down all of the walls and brings out the smiles. For the more resistive, he nuzzles his head against them and stares them in the eye, almost as if to say, "It's okay, you tried your best." This simple thing, that is goofy in and of itself, can make a huge difference in a young wrestler's life. It shows them that someone cares, and that they're not alone in their struggle.

In the end, Lionel's impact on the Peachtree Ridge Wrestling Team goes beyond just making kids smile. He has become a symbol of the team's values: hard work, determination, and compassion. He reminds us that even in the face of defeat, we can still find joy and meaning in our efforts. Yes, I know what you're thinking. Do the kids actually like it? The answer is simply this... They ask for him at **every** event. For me wearing Lionel makes me feel hot, it's not comfortable, and it most definitely isn't flattering. Not to mention that I am almost positive that I am the butt of every joke at the events but at the end of the day its for the kids. The question is, how important are your kids smiling to you? For me, it's everything!

FUN HAPPENS EVERYWHERE

Something that most people don't think about is having fun outside of the wrestling room too! These activities can provide an opportunity for athletes to bond and connect developing a strong team culture that supports individual and team success. Some examples of team building activities that coaches might consider include bowling, laser tag, watching a movie, or other group outings. These activities can be a fun way to blow off steam and build relationships, and they can also help to improve communication, trust, and team camaraderie among athletes.

I call these 'Team Nights'. I have had great success taking the kids to local event venues for our team nights. Seeking out sponsorships for these events can also help to reduce costs and make them more accessible to all athletes. By hosting 'Team Nights' that feature fun activities outside of the wrestling room, coaches can create a supportive and engaging environment that encourages athletes to stay committed to the program and to work together towards shared goals.

Ultimately, by prioritizing fun and team building in addition to technique and conditioning, coaches can create a more well-rounded and successful youth wrestling program.

"Fun is a big part of the entertainment because if you're not having fun, you're not going to enjoy the sport, and if you're not enjoying the sport, you're not going to continue to do it."
- Kyle Dake

19.

CLUB SANCTIONING AND EVENT SELECTION

If you have wrestled before or have been around wrestling on the high school or college levels then you may already be at least a little familiar with this topic. With youth programs, the options vary based on region and those options will limit your ability to select events for your program.

PART A: SANCTION YOUR CLUB

There are three main organizations who serve their respective wrestling communities. If your club has multiple options to choose from, there are several reasons why a wrestling club might choose to sanction their club through USA Wrestling, AAU, and/or Nuway. These organizations are all national wrestling governing bodies that provide support and resources for wrestling clubs, including insurance coverage, access to competitions, and coaching education.

USA WRESTLING

One reason a wrestling club might choose to sanction through USA Wrestling is the organization's strong focus on Olympic-style wrestling and developing wrestling for all ages. USA Wrestling is a national governing body for Olympic wrestling in the United States and is recognized by the International Olympic Committee. As a result, many wrestlers and clubs who are interested in competing at the highest levels of the sport, including the Olympics, may choose to sanction through USA Wrestling. Additionally USA Wrestling offers a comprehensive coaches education program for new coaches. For sanctioning events, coaches memberships, and athlete memberships, USA Wrestling is the most costly of the three options, but USA Wrestling offers a whole host of premier national level wrestling events unmatched by any other organization.

AAU

AAU (Amateur Athletic Union) is another national governing body that offers wrestling programs and events. AAU is known for its emphasis on youth sports and its focus on providing a positive and inclusive environment for athletes of all ages. Depending on your region, your local AAU clubs may not offer the Olympic styles like comparative USA clubs will. Wrestling clubs that are interested in participating in AAU events may choose to sanction through the organization in order to access its resources and programs. They offer a similar insurance policy to USA Wrestling, but their costs for athlete and coaches memberships are much cheaper. Additionally they make it really easy to get 501c3 non-profit status, tax free status, and accept tax exempt donations with one of their club membership options.

NUWAY

Nuway (National United Wrestling Association for Youth) is a third national governing body that offers wrestling programs and events. Nuway is known for its focus on providing opportunities for wrestlers to not only wrestle, but participate in other martial arts such as Ju-Jitsu as well. Clubs that are interested in participating in Nuway events may choose to sanction through the organization in order to access its resources and programs. Something that sets Nuway apart is their use of the Smoothcomp platform. While the other two organizations use products from FloSports.

PART B: PLAN YOUR EVENTS

In wrestling, there are two main types of events: individual and dual. Individual events are competitions in which a wrestler competes against one opponent at a time, while dual events involve two teams competing against each other with multiple wrestlers competing in each match.

One key difference between individual and dual events is the general structure for each. In individual events, a wrestler must solely focus on their own performance and strategy, as they are the only one competing in their match. This can be both a positive and a negative, as it allows the wrestler to focus on themselves, but it also puts a lot of pressure on them to perform well. Typically, there is a lot of downtime between matches during individual events so some kids tend to struggle to stay focused between matches. In contrast, dual events require wrestlers to not only focus on their own match, but also to be aware of the overall team score and strategy. On the youth level it is much more about cheering on their teammates. This can be a more collaborative and team-oriented approach to competition, as wrestlers must work together and support each other in order to secure a win for their team.

Another difference between individual and dual events is the level of intensity and competition. Individual events tend to be more intense, as a wrestler is directly competing against one opponent and the stakes are higher for each individual match. Dual events, on the other hand, may have a slightly lower level of intensity, as wrestlers are competing as part of a team and the focus is on the team score rather than individual victories.

BUILD YOUR SCHEDULE

Overall, both individual and dual events have their own unique challenges and benefits for youth wrestlers. When you're building your schedule, try to get a good mix of both event types. It can be unhealthy for a program to focus exclusively on individual or dual events since the needs of your kids will vary. If you're starting the program for the first time with a team of novice wrestlers, then it may be in your best interest to set up some scrimmages or duals with local teams so you can not only line up matches in advance, but prevent kids from leaving before they've really had a chance to buy in. Ultimately, both types of events can be valuable experiences for young wrestlers and can help them develop their skills and confidence on the mat.

PARENT BURNOUT IS A REAL THING

Parents are just as susceptible to burnout as your wrestlers. Wrestling tournaments take a toll on people. Especially if they are all day long. A hurdle you will have to overcome is team building to be discussed in the next chapter, but when you're building your schedule you need to build it with your families in mind. On that note, I have a few suggestions below.

— Try to aim for one event per week. Events would be any duals, individual tournaments, team building events, etc.

— Try to group your individual tournaments together in one weekend if you are planning to attend open and novice (beginner) events.

— Host a single tournament or dual every season. Your kids need to be able to compete at home. The more you do it, the better. If you can make your first event at home, it is even better! It can be a scramble, a novice, an open, or even a dual event.

— Your very first competition shouldn't be baptism by fire. That is the fastest way to lose your kids. They need to wrestle a match or two and then go home!

— Try to avoid having families out every weekend from dawn till dusk. Set a limit for any events you can. Keep your families in the building for no more than eight hours total plus weigh ins.

Ultimately, the thing you need to know is that most youth wrestling families aren't ready for the grind. I like to compare this process to farming. It is a lot of work to get a farm started. Eventually you will have a successful farm, but it takes years of sowing and learning the process to get to the point that you're successful. If you can do that, then you will start to see entire families bought in.

"Take pride in how far you have come and have faith in how far you can go."
-Michael Josephson

20.

GET RECOGNIZED

There is a time and place for everything. Promoting your youth wrestling program is an essential aspect of growing your team and attracting new athletes. With so many options available, it can be challenging to determine the most effective ways to promote your program. In this chapter, we'll explore the different approaches you can take to spread the word about your youth wrestling team, including leveraging social media platforms, running ads, establishing relationships with local news outlets, and more. By the end of this chapter, you'll have a better understanding of how to promote your program effectively and attract new athletes to your team.

DON'T SPREAD YOURSELF THIN

Your time is valuable, and it's impossible to do everything. That's why it's important to focus on one social media platform and be consistent with it. Although the social media landscape is constantly changing, Facebook is currently a great option for reaching people in your community. After creating a page, you can also join other groups with it. Consider finding a social media chair to delegate the task to. Below are descriptions of popular social media platforms, including some personal notes for your consideration.

— Facebook: A social networking platform that allows users to create a profile or pages, share updates, photos, and videos, and connect with friends and family.

— Twitter: A microblogging platform that allows users to send and read short posts known as tweets. Twitter is known for its real-time news updates and quick, concise messaging.

— Instagram: A photo and video sharing platform that allows users to share photos and videos, apply filters and effects, and connect with other users through likes, comments, and direct messages.

— TikTok: A video sharing platform that allows users to create short-form videos set to music, with a wide range of special effects and filters. TikTok is known for its viral trends and challenges.

— YouTube: A video sharing platform that allows users to upload, share, and view videos. YouTube is the second-largest search engine in the world, making it a popular destination for how-to tutorials, educational content, and entertainment.

— Mastodon: A decentralized social network that is designed to be more community-focused and ad-free than traditional social media platforms. Mastodon allows users to create their own communities, known as "instances," and connect with other users with similar interests.

While there are other social media platforms out there, these are the ones that are worth mentioning since your platform is going to serve as a method of advertising. However, knowing what to do with your platform is a problem in and of itself.

SOCIAL MEDIA IS A TOOL

Before you start posting on social media, create a plan that outlines what types of content you will post and how often you will post. This will help you stay consistent and ensure that your content is interesting and engaging. Your plan might include a mix of training tips, photos and videos of your athletes in action, updates on upcoming events, and behind-the-scenes looks at your program.

Hashtags are a great way to expand the reach of your social media posts. Using relevant hashtags that are commonly used in the wrestling community is a great way to get started. In addition to using popular hashtags, you can create your own hashtag to make it easier for people to find and follow your program. Here are some examples of commonly used hashtags in the wrestling community:

- #wrestling

- #wrestlinglife

- #wrestlingcoach

- #wrestlingfamily

- #wrestlingcommunity

- #wrestlingnation

- #wrestlingtraining

- #wrestlingtechnique

- #wrestlingmatch

- #wrestlingtournament

- #wrestlingpractice

- #wrestlingdrills

- #wrestlingmindset

- #wrestlingculture

- #wrestlingmotivation

Social media is a two-way conversation, so make sure you're engaging with your followers. Respond to comments and messages promptly, and encourage your followers to share their own experiences with your program. You can also run polls, ask for feedback, and share user-generated content to keep your followers engaged.

Leverage visual content in all of your posts. Visual content is more engaging than text-based content, so make sure you're using photos and videos in your social media posts. You can use your smartphone to take high-quality photos and videos of your athletes in action, and you edit them using free tools like Canva or Adobe Spark.

Partner with influencers to boost your visibility. Influencers are people in your community who have a large social media following and can help promote your program to a wider audience. Look for local wrestling coaches or athletes who have a strong social media presence, and reach out to see if they'd be willing to share your content or promote your program in exchange for a shoutout or other perks.

ADS AREN'T ALWAYS A BAD THING

Social media ads can be a great way to reach a wider audience beyond your current followers. The beauty of social media ads is that you can target specific groups of people based on their demographics, interests, and behaviors. This means that you can get your message in front of the right people who are most likely to be interested in your youth wrestling program.

To run social media ads, you'll need to create an account on the social media platform you want to advertise on (such as Facebook or Instagram) and set up an ad campaign. Here are the basic steps:

Choose your objective

What do you want to achieve with your ad? Do you want to increase awareness of your program, drive website traffic, or get more people to sign up for your email list? Choose the objective that aligns with your overall marketing goals.

Define your target audience

Who do you want to reach with your ad? You can choose from a range of targeting options, such as age, location, interests, behaviors, and more. Think about the characteristics of your ideal athlete and use those to guide your targeting.

Set your budget

How much money do you want to spend on your ad campaign? You can set a daily or lifetime budget for your ads, and the platform will optimize your spending to get the best results for your money.

Create your ad

Choose the format of your ad (such as a photo or video), write your ad copy, and add a call-to-action to encourage people to take action.

Launch your campaign

Once your ad is created, you can launch your campaign and start reaching your target audience. Monitor your ad's performance over time, and adjust your targeting or ad as needed to get the best results.

IT'S AN INVESTMENT

Running social media ads does require some investment of time and money, but it can be a cost-effective way to reach a wider audience and attract new athletes to your program. Remember, the key to using social media to promote your youth wrestling program is to stay consistent, engage with your followers, and provide value to your audience. With a little effort and creativity, you can use social media to build a strong online presence and attract new athletes to your program.

BE IN THE NEWS

Establishing relationships with local news outlets is an important part of promoting your youth wrestling program. By getting coverage in local newspapers, radio stations, and TV stations, you can raise awareness about your program and attract new athletes. However, building relationships with local reporters can be a challenge, especially if you're new to the area or don't have any prior experience with media outreach. Let's break it down.

Research local news outlets

Start by researching the local news outlets in your area. Look for newspapers, radio stations, and TV stations that cover sports or community events. You can also search online for local news blogs or websites that cover your area.

Identify key reporters/journalists

Once you've identified the news outlets in your area, look for reporters, journalists, or editors who cover sports or community events. Follow them on social media and read their articles to get a sense of their interests and writing style. This will help you tailor your pitch to their needs and interests.

Reach out to reporters

Once you've identified reporters who cover sports or community events, reach out to them via email or social media. Introduce yourself and your program, and let them know that you have an upcoming event or story that you think would be of interest to their readers or viewers. Be sure to include any relevant details, such as the date, time, and location of your event.

Be persistent

It's important to be persistent when reaching out to reporters. They may receive a lot of pitches every day, so don't be discouraged if you don't get an immediate response. Follow up with them a few days after your initial outreach, and be polite but persistent in your communications.

Build relationships

As you start to get coverage in local news outlets, make sure to thank the reporters who covered your program. You can also offer to be a source for future stories or events in your community. Building relationships with local reporters can help you get more coverage over time, and it can also help you establish your program as a valuable resource in your community.

Remember, when reaching out to local news outlets, it's important to be clear, concise, and relevant. Make sure your pitch is tailored to the needs and interests of the reporters you're reaching out to, and be persistent in your outreach. With a little effort and patience, you can establish valuable relationships with local news outlets and get more coverage for your youth wrestling program.

"You cannot buy engagement. You have to build engagement."
  -Tara-Nicholle Nelson

21.

BANQUETS & AWARDS

The end of season banquet is a special occasion for any wrestling team. It is an important time to reflect on the successes and challenges for the kids of the past season, celebrate individual and team achievements, and look forward to the future. Planning and organizing a banquet can be a daunting task, but with proper preparation and attention to detail, it can be a memorable and enjoyable event for all involved.

SCHEDULE THE EVENT

There are several key elements to consider when planning your end-of-season banquet. The most important step is to choose a date and venue that works for everyone. You may not get 100% participation due to spring sports and if you have multiple teams. This event will likely involve coordinating with the team's coaches, athletes, and parents to find a good time that is convenient for all attendees. Once a date has been selected, it is important to secure a venue that can accommodate your team, has all of the necessary amenities such as seating, tables, and a stage or podium. It may also be necessary to arrange for catering or other food and beverage options. If you plan far enough in advance, you may be able to get a local restaurant to help you with this as a team sponsor.

LOGISTICS MAKE IT HAPPEN

In addition to the logistics of the event, it is important to consider the program that will take place during the banquet. This should include speeches from the coaches, presentations of awards, and perhaps even a slideshow or video highlighting the team's achievements throughout the season. Something that I like to do is find a way to involve your athletes in the event itself. I typically do a team vote of some kind with a ballot box. The first time that Lionel the Lion Hat received his name was by ballot. It is entirely for giggles, but makes the kids feel like they have a part to play too. Overall, the goal is to ensure that the banquet reflects the team's collective spirit and celebrates the contributions of all of the wrestlers.

MINDFUL OF THE BUDGET

It is essential to also consider the budget and costs associated with the banquet. This may include fees for the venue, catering, and any decorations or other supplies that are needed. It may also be necessary to collect funds from attendees to cover these costs, or to seek sponsorships or donations to help offset the expense. Regardless of the budget, it is important to be mindful of costs and to prioritize the most important elements of the event while still creating a meaningful and memorable experience for all involved. Your families should leave feeling like the time and funds for the event should be more than worth it, and they should also leave excited for the next season!

AWARDS

When it comes to choosing the awards to give out at banquets, it is important to consider what you want to encourage within your program. However before we delve into the awards for the banquet, it is worth mentioning the importance of rewarding kids throughout the season for good behavior.

In my program, I implemented a program called the "Champion of the Week" award. The goal was to promote and reward positive behavior in our young wrestlers. This award was not necessarily based on wrestling performance, but rather on the wrestler's behavior both on and off the mat. We purchased a boys and a girls belt from BuildUrBelt.com for each team.

Each week, I presented a belt to the wrestler who displayed exceptional sportsmanship, work ethic, and leadership. This belt served as a constant reminder of their accomplishment and was designed to be worn to school, giving them the opportunity to show off their achievement.

The values of our program were inscribed on the belt, ensuring that the recipient understood the significance of their award. This program helped to instill a culture of positivity and good behavior within our team and helped to reinforce the values that we wanted our wrestlers to embody both on and off the mat. Want to know the best part? The kids got competitive over it!

I highly recommend implementing a similar program in your youth wrestling program. Not only does it encourage positive behavior, but it also helps to create a strong team dynamic and fosters a sense of pride in a wrestler's accomplishments. By rewarding good behavior throughout the season, you are helping to shape the overall culture of your program, which will benefit all wrestlers involved. If you have them bring it back every week, you can reuse it week to week and then ultimately turn it into another award at the end of the season!

BANQUET AWARDS

As far as the banquet goes, I would suggest having at least state placer awards, record holder awards, and most improved awards. Are you looking to promote your values through your awards? If so, then you may want to include an award for displaying the values for your program. Do you want to promote being a good student? Then maybe include an award for exceptional in-school performance. If you plan it right, you can reuse your belts from during the season for an award of your choosing. I've listed some awards to help get your ideas flowing. This isn't a concrete list, but is more of a whiteboard of ideas for you.

— Most Improved Wrestler: Awarded to the wrestler who has shown the most improvement throughout the season.

— Outstanding Wrestler: Awarded to the wrestler who has consistently performed at a high level throughout the season.

— Sportsmanship Award: Awarded to the wrestler who has shown exceptional sportsmanship and respect for their opponents and teammates.

— Leadership Award: Awarded to the wrestler who has shown outstanding leadership skills both on and off the mat.

— Academic Achievement Award: Awarded to the wrestler who has excelled academically while also participating in the sport.

— Rookie of the Year: Awarded to the first-year wrestler who has shown the most promise and potential.

— Most Dedicated Wrestler: Awarded to the wrestler who has demonstrated the most dedication and commitment to the sport throughout the season.

— Team Spirit Award: Awarded to the wrestler who has shown exceptional team spirit and enthusiasm throughout the season.

— Most Valuable Wrestler: Awarded to the wrestler who has made the biggest impact on the team's success throughout the season.

— Most Courageous Wrestler: Awarded to the wrestler who has shown exceptional courage and perseverance throughout the season.

— Hardest Worker Award: Awarded to the wrestler who has shown exceptional work ethic and dedication to improving their skills throughout the season.

— Outstanding Conditioning Award: Awarded to the wrestler who has shown exceptional conditioning and stamina on the mat.

— Ironman Award: Awarded to the wrestler who has shown exceptional durability and toughness throughout the season.

— Most Technical Wrestler: Awarded to the wrestler who has demonstrated the most technical proficiency on the mat.

— Outstanding Supporter Award: Awarded to the individual who has demonstrated exceptional support and dedication to the team throughout the season.

Expanding on the previous point, keeping records throughout the season can be a great way to track progress and recognize achievements beyond just the end-of-season banquet awards. If you are already tracking stats such as wins and pins, why not keep records of other achievements as well? For example, you could track things like attendance, improvement in technique, or even acts of sportsmanship.

By keeping records and recognizing these achievements throughout the season, you not only encourage your wrestlers to strive for excellence but also create a culture of positivity and support. It shows your wrestlers that you are invested in their growth and development beyond just their performance on the mat.

These records could be kept in a simple spreadsheet or even on a whiteboard in the wrestling room. Make sure to share these accomplishments with the team regularly, whether it be during practice or before a match. This recognition and positive reinforcement can go a long way in boosting morale and encouraging a team-oriented mindset.

— Takedown Record Award: Awarded to the wrestler who has recorded the most takedowns during the season.

— Escape Record Award: Awarded to the wrestler who has recorded the most escapes during the season.

— Reversal Record Award: Awarded to the wrestler who has recorded the most reversals during the season.

— Near Fall Record Award: Awarded to the wrestler who has recorded the most back points during the season.

— Pin Record Award: Awarded to the wrestler who has recorded the most pins during the season.

— Tech Fall Record Award: Awarded to the wrestler who has recorded the most tech falls during the season.

Each year, our program recognizes two special awards that highlight and encourage excellence both on and off the wrestling mat. The awards include the esteemed **Little Lion Award** and the prestigious **Academic All-American Award**.

The Little Lion Award is a cherished honor within our program, and it is presented to a wrestler who demonstrates outstanding commitment, dedication, and sportsmanship. The recipient receives a unique and unforgettable prize — a personalized belt with their picture and award definition that serves as a constant reminder of their hard work and achievement.

The Academic All American Award is a concept that originated from esteemed coach, Ken Chertow, whom I have had the privilege of knowing for more than 20 years. During my time attending his camps, I was inspired by his Academic All-American Awards, which required us to submit a short essay for consideration.

Winning the award each year was a significant accomplishment for me, as Coach Chertow emphasized the importance of excelling in both the classroom and on the mat.

This belt represents that the honoree is not just an outstanding student in academics and athletics, but a highly respected leader among his peers, with a commitment to team goals and pride in Peachtree Ridge, and whose character sets an example for everyone on this team to emulate.

As a youth program director, I have adopted this same idea, and every year at our banquet, we celebrate the accomplishments of our Academic All American award recipients. Entrants have to submit their grades with a parent signature and then write an essay to respond to a prompt:

What is something that you have learned from wrestling? How has what you learned made you a better student in the classroom?

Winners are presented with a specially designed T-shirt that showcases their achievement and our program's logo; we promote the value of being a well-rounded student-athlete. This investment not only fosters character development but also serves as free advertising, highlighting our support for academic excellence in addition to wrestling prowess.

I highly recommend implementing unique awards like these in your program to recognize and encourage well-rounded development in your wrestlers. By doing so, you not only honor and motivate individual achievements but also foster a culture of excellence and respect within your program.

"Awards can give you a tremendous amount of encouragement to keep getting better, no matter how young or old you are."
- Alan Alda

22.

AVOID ATHLETE BURNOUT

Athlete burnout is a common issue that can affect athletes of all ages, including kids who participate in wrestling. It is important to recognize the signs of burnout and take steps to prevent it, as burnout can lead to decreased performance, even to the point when wrestlers quit the sport with a bad taste in their mouths.

IDENTIFY

Identifying burnout in young wrestlers can be a challenging task, as the symptoms are often subtle and can be attributed to other factors. However, recognizing the early signs of burnout is crucial in preventing more serious burnout and helping the wrestler to stay motivated and engaged in the sport.

Some signs of burnout in young wrestlers include a loss of interest in the sport, a decrease in performance, and a negative attitude toward training and competition. Burnout can also manifest itself in physical symptoms such as fatigue, lack of energy, and decreased immunity. Coaches and parents should be on the lookout for these signs and take them seriously.

One way to identify burnout is to keep an open line of communication with the wrestlers. Coaches should check in with their athletes regularly to gauge their level of interest and enthusiasm for the sport. This can be done informally during practice or more formally through one-on-one meetings. Similarly, parents should have open and honest conversations with their children about how they are feeling and what they are experiencing in the sport.

Another way to identify burnout is to look for changes in behavior. For example, a wrestler who was previously very social and outgoing may become more withdrawn and isolated, indicating a lack of motivation or interest in the sport. Coaches and parents should also be aware of changes in sleep patterns, eating habits, and academic performance, as these can all be indicators of burnout.

By staying vigilant and aware of these signs, coaches and parents can take proactive steps to prevent burnout and ensure that young wrestlers stay motivated and engaged in the sport.

BALANCE

Preventing burnout in wrestlers requires a balanced approach to the sport that emphasizes fun and enjoyment alongside commitment to training and competition. Coaches can help their athletes avoid burnout by encouraging them to take breaks during practice, especially during long, intense sessions, and to focus on the fundamentals of wrestling without getting bogged down in the pressure to win.

One way to prevent burnout is to focus on scoring points and to let the wins come naturally. Young wrestlers who are overly focused on winning can quickly become overwhelmed and lose their love of the sport. Instead of pressuring athletes to win, coaches can teach them to enjoy the process of learning new techniques and strategies, and to appreciate the satisfaction that comes from improving their skills. This approach can help athletes stay motivated and engaged in the sport, while also preventing the mental and physical exhaustion that can lead to burnout.

Coaches can also help wrestlers avoid burnout by creating a positive and supportive team culture. This can include activities outside of practice, such as team-building events, group workouts, and social outings. By creating a sense of camaraderie and support, athletes can feel more connected to their teammates and to the sport, which can help them stay motivated and engaged even during difficult times. Coaches can also encourage athletes to take breaks and to step back from wrestling when they feel overwhelmed, They can encourage them to focus on other activities that bring them joy and fulfillment. This can help prevent burnout and ensure that athletes continue to grow and develop both on and off the mat.

SUPPORT

Creating a positive and supportive culture within the wrestling program is a key factor in preventing burnout in young athletes. Coaches should check in with their wrestlers regularly to ensure that they are feeling supported and motivated. This can be done through one-on-one meetings or even casual conversations before or after practice. It is important for coaches to create an environment where wrestlers feel comfortable sharing their thoughts and feelings, so that they can identify potential burnout and address it before it becomes a bigger issue.

In addition, coaches should encourage parents to be supportive and positive towards their wrestlers. This means that parents should avoid adding additional pressure and stress to their child by focusing on wins and losses. Rather, they should focus on their child's progress and celebrate their child's achievements no matter how big or small. I set my expectations early in the season with my parents, and I would encourage you to do the same. There is no one who will make your wrestlers quit the sport faster than their parents. I tell my parents to be parents. Let the coaches coach. I know this is pretty obvious, but I hold my parents accountable for this. When their kids come off the mat and come to the stands, I want them to give them praise and tell them how amazing they did regardless of how they actually performed. At the end of the day, your coaches should set clear expectations for parents at the beginning of the season and hold them accountable throughout the year.

During practice, coaches should also incorporate breaks and fun activities to keep the wrestlers engaged and motivated. These breaks can include games or other team-building activities that encourage social interaction and positive relationships among the team. Coaches should also focus on the process of scoring points and not solely on winning. By creating a focus on scoring points, coaches can help wrestlers to see the progress they are making and build confidence in their abilities.

Ultimately, creating a positive and supportive environment is the key to preventing burnout and keeping wrestlers engaged and motivated. By checking in with athletes regularly, setting clear expectations for parents, incorporating breaks during practice, and focusing on the process of scoring points, coaches can create a culture that promotes healthy development and long-term success.

"You're either winning or you're learning. There is no losing here."
-Tre Horton

23.

OLYMPIC STYLES

Freestyle and Greco-Roman wrestling are two styles of wrestling that are popular at the international level and offer a number of advantages for Folkstyle wrestlers who are looking to improve their skills and compete at a higher level. Most traditional programs end around March, but the Olympic styles provide you an opportunity to keep the kids engaged while ditching the monotony.

WHAT ARE THE OLYMPIC STYLES?

Freestyle and Greco-Roman wrestling are the two international styles of wrestling that are highly popular and widely recognized. While both styles share some similarities, they also have some notable differences.

In freestyle wrestling, the goal is to turn your opponent and not expose your back. Points are awarded for actions such as takedowns, turns, and exposure. The wrestler with the most points at the end of the match wins. Freestyle wrestling also allows for more wrestling on the feet compared to folkstyle wrestling, which requires wrestlers to start in a referee's position. This makes freestyle wrestling a more fast-paced and dynamic style of wrestling.

Greco-Roman wrestling, on the other hand, is unique in that it prohibits the use of the legs in offense and defense. This means that only upper-body techniques can be used in a match. Like freestyle wrestling, the goal is to score points by throwing your opponent, pinning them to the mat, or executing a takedown.

In both freestyle and Greco-Roman wrestling, wrestlers must be highly skilled in throws and holds as well as top and bottom positions. They must be able to execute a variety of moves and have quick reflexes to avoid their opponent's attempts. By learning and practicing these different styles of wrestling, wrestlers can develop a more well-rounded and diverse skill set that can benefit them in any wrestling competition.

For wrestlers who are used to folkstyle wrestling, the transition to the Olympic styles may require some adjustments in their techniques and strategies. The differences in rules and scoring can make a significant impact on how matches are approached. By taking part in freestyle and Greco-Roman wrestling classes and matches, wrestlers can gain valuable experience and skills that will help them compete at a higher level.

Overall, the Olympic styles of wrestling offer a unique and exciting opportunity for wrestlers to challenge themselves and learn new techniques. They provide a great opportunity for wrestlers to expand their skill sets, and they can be a great way to keep kids engaged in the sport during the spring and summer months.

WHO DO YOU OFFER THIS TO?

When it comes to offering freestyle and Greco-Roman wrestling, the age group you choose to invite to participate will depend on a number of factors, including your comfort level, the skill level of your athletes, and the availability of other wrestling programs in your area.

Some wrestling programs offer freestyle and Greco to all age groups, from youth to high school. This can be a great opportunity to expose younger athletes to different styles of wrestling and help them develop a more well-rounded skill set. However, it can also be challenging to work with athletes of different ages and skill levels, and you may need to modify your practice plans and coaching strategies to accommodate different needs.

Other programs may choose to limit their spring wrestling programs to middle school and high school athletes. This can be a good option if you want to focus on more competitive wrestling and work with athletes who already have a solid foundation in the sport.

If you're just starting out with freestyle and Greco, it may be in your best interest to limit your program to older and more experienced athletes. This will allow you to focus on coaching and developing the fundamentals of the different styles of wrestling without having to worry about the challenges of working with younger or less-experienced athletes.

Another option is to partner with a nearby college wrestling program to make your practices available to their wrestlers.

This can be a great way to offer additional training opportunities to your athletes, and it can also help to build relationships between your program and the college program.

No matter what age group you choose to offer freestyle and Greco to, it's important to communicate your goals and expectations with your athletes and their parents. Let them know what to expect from the practices and competitions, and be open to feedback and suggestions for improvement. With the right approach and a supportive coaching staff, you can offer a fun and challenging freestyle and Greco program that helps your athletes develop their skills and reach their full potential.

HOW OFTEN DO YOU PRACTICE?

When deciding on a practice schedule for your freestyle and Greco-Roman wrestling program, it's important to consider the competitive level you are aiming for and the availability of your wrestlers. Here are some practical examples to consider:

Competitive Olympic Season

If your goal is to have a competitive season, I would recommended to practice at least three times a week. You should consider having two days dedicated to freestyle practice and one day for Greco-Roman wrestling. For instance, you could have practice on Monday, Wednesday, and Friday. The first two days of practice can focus on freestyle wrestling, and the last day of the week can focus on Greco-Roman wrestling. This practice schedule will allow your wrestlers to develop skills and techniques in both Olympic styles and help them prepare for competitions.

A Season for Learning Experience

If you're just looking to keep your wrestlers engaged and learning during the spring season, it may be sufficient to practice once a week. For instance, you could practice on Sunday afternoons for a few hours. During these practices, you can introduce wrestlers to new techniques, review existing skills, and offer a fun, learning experience for all. While this may not prepare your wrestlers for competitive Olympic-style wrestling, it will still help them improve their overall wrestling abilities and keep them engaged in the sport during the off-season.

Availability of Wrestlers

It's important to consider the availability of your wrestlers when deciding on a practice schedule. If your wrestlers are involved in other sports during the spring, it may be challenging to schedule regular practices. In such a case, you may want to consider offering more flexible practice schedules. For instance, you could have one or two regular practice days a week, but allow wrestlers to attend whenever they are available. This will enable wrestlers to participate in other activities and still have an opportunity to practice Olympic-style wrestling.

Combination of Competitive and Learning Experience Season

If you want to offer a combination of a competitive and learning experience season, you could consider having two practice days per week. For example, you could practice on Tuesday and Thursday evenings for two hours each. During these practices, you could focus on freestyle and Greco-Roman wrestling, respectively. On the first day, you could introduce new techniques and work on improving existing ones. On the second day, you could apply those techniques in a more competitive environment, giving wrestlers a chance to practice Olympic-style wrestling against one another.

Your practice schedule for freestyle and Greco-Roman wrestling will depend on your goals, the availability of your wrestlers, and the level of competitiveness you are aiming to achieve. It's important to be flexible and considerate of your wrestlers' needs while still offering them a fun and rewarding wrestling experience.

"It is not the mountain we conquer, but ourselves."
- Sir Edmund Hillary

24.

WRAP UP

Congratulations, you've made it to the end of this book! Whether you're a new wrestling coach, a parent of a young wrestler thinking about starting a wrestling program, or an experienced coach looking for new ideas, I hope you've found the information in this book to be helpful and inspiring. As you continue to work with your wrestlers, remember that coaching is an ongoing process, and there is always more to learn and improve upon. Here are some final thoughts to keep in mind:

Focus on the process, not just the outcome

Focusing on the process is essential to achieving success in wrestling. While it's natural to have a desire to win, it's crucial to keep in mind that winning is just one part of the sport. The true essence of wrestling lies in the process of learning and improving, whether it's mastering a new technique or building stamina and endurance through rigorous training. Encourage your wrestlers to embrace the process of growth and improvement, rather than being solely fixated on winning.

By focusing on the process, wrestlers can improve their skills and build their confidence, which can help them become better athletes and more well-rounded individuals. When athletes focus solely on winning, they often become overly stressed and anxious, which can affect their performance on the mat. Instead of fixating on the outcome, encourage your wrestlers to enjoy the journey, embrace the challenges, and focus on the steps they need to take to reach their goals.

It's important to remember that progress and growth take time.

Encourage your wrestlers to set realistic goals and to celebrate each small victory along the way. By breaking down the process into manageable steps, wrestlers can develop a sense of achievement and progress that can help keep them motivated and engaged in the sport. Whether it's learning a new technique, mastering a challenging drill, or simply showing up to practice each day, every effort counts towards the ultimate goal of becoming a better wrestler.

Ultimately, focusing on the process can help wrestlers develop a deeper appreciation for the sport of wrestling and the journey of growth and improvement. When they understand that success is not just about winning but also about the journey of growth, they can approach each challenge with a sense of purpose and a positive attitude. By instilling this mindset in your wrestlers, you can help them develop the skills and confidence they need to become successful wrestlers and well-rounded individuals.

Embrace challenge and change

Embracing challenge and change is a fundamental aspect of the wrestling journey. The sport is full of challenges, from tough opponents to learning new techniques and strategies, and each obstacle presents an opportunity for growth and improvement.

Wrestling can be a rollercoaster of highs and lows, but it's important to remember that every challenge is a chance to become a better wrestler and a stronger person.

As wrestlers, it's essential to be open to change and to embrace it as a necessary part of the journey. Wrestling is constantly evolving, and staying ahead of the curve requires a willingness to learn new techniques, adapt to new rules and regulations, and embrace new training methods. By doing so, we can stay on the cutting edge of the sport and give ourselves the best chance of success.

Challenges and changes can be difficult to handle, and they can be particularly daunting for young wrestlers. However, by approaching these obstacles with a growth mindset, we can turn them into opportunities for development and growth. Rather than shying away from difficult situations, we should view them as chances to test our limits, learn from our mistakes, and push ourselves to be better.

Ultimately, the wrestling journey is about much more than wins and losses. It's about building resilience, gaining confidence, and learning to embrace challenge and change. By doing so, we can become not only better wrestlers, but better people as well. So, as you continue your wrestling journey, remember to stay open to new experiences, be willing to learn and grow, and never shy away from a challenge.

Stay organized

Staying organized is not just important for being an effective coach, but it also helps to reduce stress and promote a healthy work-life balance. There are several practical steps that you can take to stay organized and on top of your coaching duties.

One of the first steps is to use a planner or calendar to keep track of your schedule. This can include practices, competitions, meetings, and other important events. You can use a physical planner or an online tool such as Google Calendar to ensure that you don't miss any important dates or deadlines.

In addition to keeping track of your schedule, it's important to prioritize your tasks. Determine which tasks are most urgent or important and tackle them first. This can help you avoid getting overwhelmed and ensure that you stay on track with your coaching responsibilities.

Another key aspect of staying organized is delegating responsibilities. Don't be afraid to enlist the help of assistant coaches, team managers, or parents to help with tasks such as transportation, equipment management, or fundraising. Delegating responsibilities can help to reduce your workload and allow you to focus on the tasks that require your attention.

Finally, it's important to develop a system for managing paperwork and communication. This can include creating folders for important documents such as team rosters, medical forms, and competition schedules. You may also want to consider using communication tools such as email or text messaging to keep parents and athletes informed about important updates or changes.

By staying organized and on top of your coaching duties, you can help to ensure that your athletes have a positive and rewarding experience in wrestling. Taking the time to plan and prioritize your tasks can help to reduce stress, increase productivity, and ultimately lead to a more successful season.

Stay positive

Staying organized is not just important for being an effective coach, but it also helps to reduce stress and promote a healthy work-life balance. There are several practical steps that you can take to stay organized and on top of your coaching duties.

One of the first steps is to use a planner or calendar to keep track of your schedule. This can include practices, competitions, meetings, and other important events. You can use a physical planner or an online tool such as Google Calendar to ensure that you don't miss any important dates or deadlines. Additionally, it is important to set realistic expectations with parents and to communicate with them regularly. Be honest about the time commitment and physical demands of the sport, as well as the potential for setbacks and disappointments. Encourage parents to focus on their child's growth and development, rather than just on winning or losing. By setting realistic expectations and fostering a positive, supportive relationship with parents, you can create a healthier and more productive environment for your wrestlers.

In addition, set achievable program goals that align with your team's abilities and strengths. These goals should be challenging, but also realistic and attainable. Make sure to involve your wrestlers in the goal-setting process and communicate regularly with them about their progress. Celebrate their achievements, no matter how small, and encourage them to learn from their mistakes and setbacks.

Remember that your role as a coach goes beyond teaching wrestling techniques and strategies. You are a mentor and a leader, and your attitude and approach can have a profound impact on your wrestlers' experiences and outcomes. By staying positive, setting realistic expectations with parents, and setting achievable program goals, you can create a culture of success, growth, and development for your wrestlers both on and off the mat.

Stay engaged with the wrestling community

Staying engaged with the wrestling community is essential for any coach who wants to succeed in the sport. By attending wrestling events, you can not only show support for your team, but also network with other coaches and gain new insights into coaching techniques and strategies.

One great way to stay connected with the wrestling community is to become a member of the National Wrestling Coaches Association (NWCA). The NWCA provides a wealth of resources for coaches, including training programs, coaching tips, and access to online forums and discussions. Additionally, the NWCA hosts an annual convention every summer, which provides an opportunity to connect with other coaches and learn from some of the best minds in the sport.

Another valuable resource for wrestling coaches is FCA Wrestling, a faith-based organization that provides coaching clinics, training programs, and other resources for coaches who want to help their athletes grow not only as wrestlers, but also as individuals. FCA Wrestling emphasizes character development, spiritual growth, and leadership, and provides coaches with the tools they need to inspire their athletes to be their best both on and off the mat.

Local USA Wrestling programs are another great organization for coaches to get involved with. As one of the national governing bodies for amateur wrestling in the United States, USA Wrestling provides coaches with access to training programs, certification programs, and coaching resources.

By staying engaged with the wrestling community and taking advantage of these resources, coaches can stay up-to-date on the latest coaching techniques and strategies, and help their athletes achieve their full potential. Whether it's through attending events, joining organizations like the NWCA or FCA Wrestling, or participating in training programs through USA Wrestling, there are many ways for coaches to stay connected and continue to grow as coaches and as individuals.

CHALLENGE TIME

It's the last one! Take some time to reflect on your experience reading this book. What were your favorite parts? What did you learn that you can apply to your own coaching or parenting? What questions do you still have? What topics do you want to learn more about?

_____

_____

_____

_____

_____

_____

_____

_____

_____

I hope this book has provided you with a solid foundation for starting the wrestling program your community needs. There is nothing as rewarding as coaching young wrestlers. Whether you're a seasoned pro or just getting started, remember that coaching is a journey, and there is always more to learn and explore. Keep an open mind, stay positive, and always put the needs of your wrestlers first. With dedication, hard work, and a commitment to growth, you can help your young wrestlers achieve their goals and develop into confident, skilled, and successful athletes. I hope your journey is as successful and rewarding as mine.

If you enjoyed reading this book, please take some time to leave a review where you bought it!

Thank you for reading!

APPENDIX A.

HARD TRUTHS

As a youth wrestling program director or coach, it can be challenging to navigate the ups and downs of building and maintaining a successful program. That's why it's important to seek advice and guidance from other coaches who have been through the same struggles.

In this appendix, I've asked several coaches to share their hard truths about running a wrestling program. These are coaches who have been in the trenches, experienced the highs and lows, and learned important lessons along the way.

IF YOU COULD GO BACK AND TELL YOURSELF ONE THING, ONE HARD TRUTH ABOUT RUNNING A WRESTLING PROGRAM, WHAT WOULD IT BE?

"You will always care more about what you are doing than the parents of your program will."

- Tre Horton

"Do it for the kids and be very selective of who you surround your kids and yourself with."

- Willie Hilton, Sly Fox Wrestling Club

"Wrestling is supposed to be about more than just learning moves on the mat. Wrestling is supposed to teach you how to work hard, overcome adversity, and build character through the wins and loses."

- Jason Powers, Jackson County High School

"You are right. Trust yourself sooner."

- Lee Roper, University of Northern Iowa

"Head coaching is going to take more time than you will ever realize to build a championship program. Be patient."

- Jared Harris, Peachtree Ridge High School

"If you are going to coach youth sports never lose sight of making sure the fun stays first and foremost! Anything that takes away from the enthusiasm of the athlete stifles growth and slows the natural progression of learning. These detractors can take many forms, including but not limited to; overbearing parents, to much competition, weight cutting, and putting winning first over learning. Be a Shepard to your flock and keep those distractors of what is best for your flock at bay and your kids and your program will thrive!"

- Jeff Ragan, Woodward Academy

"Most people don't know how to run a business, and the hard truth is that running a wrestling program is exactly like running a business. You have to focus on cash flow to support the programs infrastructure to cover the costs and develop opportunities that underfunded programs can't afford to do; you need a business plan."

- Dustin Kawa, owner of Takedown Sportswear, The Wrestling Academy

"Be flexible with your methods, but not your values."

- Rob Tate, Queens University

"You have to understand that half of the youth season is going to be baby sitting. Embrace it and find a way to invest in the kids you know will benefit the most and return every year."

- Donovan Padrone, Level Up Wrestling Club

"You gotta create the best environment where the kids will want to continue to wrestle. Retention is paramount."

- Jim Gassman, Mountain View High School

"You and your Coaches will always care more than the parents."

- Mason Patton, North Hall High School

"If you can't get off bottom, then you are just average."

-Brian Tacto, Banks County Youth Wrestling

"You will never have 100% control 100% of the time. You will face factors that you can control and others you cannot. Be smart about where you focus your energy."

- Donnell Bradley, Greenbriar High School

"You have to prepare to beat the other wrestler and the official so that when there is a controversial call and the parents are upset, you can share that you've already prepared for it."

- Rocco Cash, South Paulding High School

"You will make a lot of mistakes. Learn from them."
- Dillan Schouw, owner Snapdown Designs, Holy Innocence

"If you are going to coach young kids, be prepared to give a lot of hugs."
- Joe Croce, Team Georgia Kids Director, Woodstock Youth Wrestling

Proverbs 22:6 Train up a child in the way he should go; even when he is old he will not depart from it.
- Billy Pope, South Forsyth Wrestling Club

"It is important that you are doing this with the sole purpose of helping others. Nothing more and nothing less. If it is about money, pats on the back, ego, or success, then you are going down the wrong path. You will spend years or even decades developing athletes with limited tangible returns other than the development of your wrestlers. Be prepared to be the person that gives everything and receives only the work of your athletes back."
- Blake Maffei, Reverence Wrestling Club

"Invest in the KIDS rather than winning titles. Your relationships will be much, much, stronger."
- Ryan Millhof, Collins Hill High School

"CULTURE MATTERS! Developing your culture and recruiting the RIGHT fit is just as important as winning. Be willing to sacrifice winning to teach young people life lessons that they can take with them when they leave your program. "
- **Tyler Smith, Brewton Parker College**

"Don't focus so much on developing great wrestlers that you neglect developing Godly men. Great leadership characteristics shouldn't be confined to 7 minutes on a mat, but those 7 minutes are crucial to developing a lifelong commitment to being a Godly leader."
- **Patrick James, Truett McConnell University**

"Kids don't choose a club. Their parents do, and to this end the key to building a great club is to get the parents on your side. You need to take advantage of their enthusiasm and make them partners not adversaries. This is probably the toughest part of coaching but also the most important, particularly for a young coach."
- **Robert Koll, Stanford University**

"Train the mind, the body will follow. You have to train the minds of your coaches, parents, athletes, and boosters to have a successful program."
- **Sean Acree, Paulding County Wrestling**

"To be a good coach, we must embrace our players and help them work through their struggles rather than just comforting them, as this can be a valuable learning journey for the long game. By teaching a child to understand their emotions and work through them, they can learn to handle losing and become more resilient."

- Weylin Beavers, West Forsyth Wrestling Club

"One of the most difficult parts of coaching is teaching kids how to be there own worst critic. Nobody likes hearing from others that they've done something wrong or made a mistake. However, teaching athletes to learn from their mistakes, take risks and then learn from their losses is crucial."

- Peter Yates, Teknique Wrestling Club

"No task is beneath you. It is not about you anymore, it's about what you can do for YOUR team."

- Cole Manion, Life University

"No one cares like you. Stop acting like the world is against you. Love the kids and everything else will work out."

- Othello Johnson, UNC Pembroke

"You will have more lows, then highs in coaching. If everyone is not rowing in the same direction, you will not reach your goals. Push everyone to be all in."

- Jake Britt, Montreat College

"Belief. If a coach does not believe then how can they expect an athlete to believe. It requires honesty on both sides."
- **Stacy Davis, Holy Innocence**

"Everyone that is great, works hard. Not everyone that works hard is great. Focus on the relationships."
- **Hunter Gamble, UTC Chattanooga**

"Encourage your wrestlers to surrender the outcome to God and glorify Him by wrestling the best they possibly can. If we learn to let go of our worry about the outcome and instead focus on what we can control (attitude, effort, intensity), then the outcome is much more likely to be favorable."
- **Denver Stonecheck, Cornerstone University**

"Start your season with basic training for parents. They all want to be mini coaches, and they need to know how to act as wrestling parents to be their kids biggest fans. Having a character coach for wrestlers and parents is just as important as having a head coach in a club. Proverbs 9:10"
- **Bill Gifford, FCA Georgia Director**

"There is no one size fits all approach to building a wrestling club. You have to examine the needs, assets, and limitations of the families that you are serving - and SERVING is the key word."
- **Jamey Ledford, Whitefield Academy**

APPENDIX B.

THANK YOU

The following individuals have had a profound impact on my life, serving as mentors and coaches during my journey as a wrestling athlete and coach. Their guidance and teachings have played a crucial role in shaping me into the person I am today. While your list of influencers may differ from mine, it is important to express gratitude to those who have made a significant difference in your life. Coaching is often a thankless profession, and acknowledging the efforts of those who have supported you can go a long way.

Whether these guys took me to practice, provided opportunities that I couldn't have had anywhere else, stayed after practices to work with me, or answered the phone when I had questions about coaching. These are the people who shaped me to be the man I am today.

Christopher Peterson
Cameron Thurmond
Jason Holcombe
Cliff Ramos
Jason Blalock
Willie Hilton
Plamen Paskalev
Doug Thurmond
Jason Powers
Dustin Kawa
Sean Page
Arturo Holmes
Roger Powers
Bud Hennebaul
Charlie Morris
Allen Spry
Jeb Stewart
Josh Porter
Jake Brumbelow
Daryk Cochran
Dillan Schouw
Anthony Flatt
Randy Bortles
Andy Nelson
Zak Moore
Scott Brown

Marcus Moulder
Bazell Partridge
Jared Harris
Ken Chertow
Othello Johnson
Omi Acosta
Brandon Slay
Jeff Ragan
Daniel Sinnott
Jeff Bedard
Joseph Guiler
Richard Schumacer
Bill Gifford
Mark Moore
Joe Croce
Kendall Love
Shawn Fields
Sean Moistner
Scott Byers
Marty Robinson
Matthew Moulder
Craig Cothern
Jason Griner
Chris Maclafferty
Nicholas Distasio
David Roman

I want to express my profound gratitude to the mentors and coaches who have played a pivotal role in my journey as a wrestling athlete and coach. Their guidance, support, and teachings have molded me into the person I am today. If I have inadvertently missed someone from my list of influencers, please know that your contribution is equally valued and appreciated.

I hope that you take a moment yourself to take a moment to honor and express your gratitude to those who have supported and shaped you. Remember that the journey of growth and learning is ongoing, and the impact of these influential figures continues to resonate in our lives, inspiring us to strive for excellence every day.

INDEX OF DEFINITIONS

Affirmation Statement: A positive statement or mantra used to build confidence and motivation, often used in sports psychology or coaching.

Athletic Director: The person responsible for overseeing the athletic programs at a school or institution.

Assistant Coaches: Individuals who assist the Head Coaches in providing instruction, guidance, and support to athletes in a sport.

Board of Directors: A group of people who oversee the management of an organization, including decisions about policies, finances, and operations.

Burnout: A state of mental, emotional, and physical exhaustion caused by prolonged stress and overwork, leading to a decline in performance and motivation.

Coaches: Individuals who provide instruction, guidance, and support to athletes in a sport.

Coaching Staff: The group of coaches responsible for leading and training a team or program.

Communication: The exchange of information and ideas between individuals or groups.

Conditioning: Training focused on developing an athlete's physical fitness, strength, and endurance.

Dual Tournaments: A type of wrestling tournament where teams compete against each other in a series of dual matches.

Drilling: Practicing and repeating specific techniques or skills, often done in a structured and repetitive manner to build muscle memory and improve performance.

Emergency Preparedness: The process of preparing and planning for emergencies or unexpected events, such as injuries or severe weather.

Fundraising Chair: Responsible for organizing fundraisers.

Girls Wrestling: The practice of wrestling for girls or female athletes, including the development of girls wrestling programs and competitions.

Goals: A specific target or achievement that is desired or intended, often used to guide training and development in athletics.

Head Coaches: Responsible for running practices, implementing the curriculum, and communicating the needs of their team to the Board.

High School Liaison: Advocates for the youth program interests when attending the High School Board meetings.

Individual Tournaments: A type of wrestling tournament where individual wrestlers compete against each other in their respective weight classes.

Junior Coaches: High school wrestlers that contribute to the youth program.

Leadership: The ability to inspire, motivate, and guide others towards a common goal or vision, often demonstrated by coaches and team captains.

Manager Coordinator: Recruits and manages team managers and acts as a goto for team moms.

Managers: Responsible for tasks such as keeping score or collecting uniforms.

Medical Supplies: Equipment and materials used for treating injuries and providing medical care, often kept on hand during practices and competitions.

Off-Season Training: Training and conditioning that occurs outside of the traditional competitive season, often used to maintain or improve skills and fitness.

Open individual tournaments: Wrestling competitions that are open to all wrestlers, regardless of their level of experience or skill.

Parent Involvement: The participation and support of parents in a youth wrestling program, often including volunteering, fundraising, and attendance at practices and competitions.

Practice Planning: The process of organizing and structuring wrestling practices, often including warm-up drills, skill-building exercises, and conditioning.

President/Chair/Director: Key leader for the youth board responsible for organizing and providing leadership oversight.

Program Development: The process of creating and building a successful wrestling program, including recruiting athletes, developing coaches, and establishing a team culture.

Scheduling: The organization and management of practice and competition schedules, often involving coordination with other teams and facilities.

Secretary: Responsible for taking meeting minutes and keeping documents organized.

Social Media: Online platforms and tools used for communication, marketing, and community-building, often used by wrestling programs to promote their team and connect with fans and supporters.

Strength Training: Exercises and activities used to build and improve muscular strength and endurance, often including weightlifting, resistance training, and bodyweight exercises.

Technique: The specific skills and movements used in wrestling, often developed through drilling and repetition.

Team Mom - Coordinates snacks and banquets. Communicates necessary information to their relevant teams.

Tournaments: Competitive events in which wrestlers compete against athletes from other teams, often involving multiple matches and brackets.

Treasurer - Responsible for creating and balancing budgets and managing board finances.

Values - A person's principles or standards of behavior, often influenced by their culture, religion, upbringing, and life experiences. In the context of wrestling, values may include concepts such as discipline, respect, hard work, sportsmanship, and teamwork. Coaches and programs may prioritize certain values to promote a positive culture and help athletes develop character and leadership skills.

Volunteer Coordinator - Coordinates volunteers for events.

Volunteer Management: The coordination and recruitment of volunteers to support a wrestling program, including tasks such as coaching, fundraising, and event management.

Wrestling Culture: The values, traditions, and norms that define a wrestling program and community, often emphasizing discipline, respect, and hard work.

ABOUT THE AUTHOR

 Tre Horton carries over twenty years of experience in the sport of wrestling as a student, athlete, and a coach. He is currently serving as the Wrestling Director for Peachtree Ridge Youth Athletic Association and as an Assistant Coach at Life University. He is also the owner and host of the Wrestling Core Podcast designed to give wrestlers everything they need to be successful in one place. He is imbued with a passion for the sport having extensive coaching experience at the youth, high school, and college levels. He has coached multiple state placers, All-Americans, and National Champions on all levels, and has received multiple awards for his outstanding coaching skills. He has served as the main point of contact for the launching of many clubs and provided valuable insight to existing clubs to foster success. In addition, he built the largest youth wrestling program in Gwinnett County, the largest county in Georgia, in two years. Tre wrestled with impressive results at Peachtree Ridge High School and finished his extensive competitive career at Brewton-Parker College. He holds USA Wrestling Bronze & Copper certifications and has completed the NWCA College Coaching Leadership Academy.

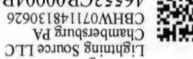